More related titles

Getting Free Publicity
The secrets of successful press relations

'For small companies, clubs, churches or charities, this step-by-step manual takes you right through from who you should target to what journalists are looking for.' – **The Bookseller**

100 Ways to Make Your Business a Success
A resource book for small business managers

'No waffle, no preaching, just straightforward advice written in an unfussy, no bulls..t manner. What a nice change.' – **K Trimble, Gaelkat Ltd**

Successful Seminar Selling
The ultimate small business guide to boosting sales and profits through seminars and workshops

'This book is ideal for small business owners as it reveals one of the most profitable ways of promoting your company – seminar selling.' – **Digby Jones, Director-General, Confederation of British Industry**

howtobooks
3 Newtec Place, Magdalen Road, Oxford OX4 1RE, United Kingdom
Tel: (01865) 793806. Fax: (01865) 248780
info@howtobooks.co.uk www.howtobooks.co.uk

THE POCKET
MEDIA
COACH

**The handy guide to getting
your message across on
TV, radio or in print**

ALAN STEVENS

howtobooks

Published by How To Books Ltd
3 Newtec Place, Magdalen Road
Oxford OX4 1RE, United Kingdom
Tel: (01865) 793806. Fax: (01865) 248780
info@howtobooks.co.uk
www.howtobooks.co.uk

British Library Cataloguing in Publication Data
A catalogue record for this book is available from the British Library.

Cover design by Baseline Arts Ltd, Oxford
Produced for How T Books by Deer Park Productions, Tavistock, Devon
Typeset by Baseline Arts Ltd, Oxford
Printed and bound by Cromwell Press, Trowbridge, Wiltshire

NOTE: The material contained in this book is set out in good faith for general
guidance and no liability can be accepted for loss or expense incurred as a
result of relying in particular circumstances on statements made in the book.
The laws and regulations are complex and liable to change, and readers
should check the current position with the relevant authorities before
making personal arrangements.

Contents

About the author

Alan Stevens CMIPR MPSA CITP MBCS

Alan is a media coach, broadcaster, PR expert, professional speaker and writer. His company (www.mediacoach.co.uk), provides individuals and organisations with the skills to communicate more effectively on radio, TV, in print and in front of an audience. He has made over 1,000 radio and TV appearances, both as a presenter and an expert interviewee. He has been quoted in every national UK newspaper, and many magazines, as well as writing articles for numerous business journals.

During a 21-year career at Consumers' Association, he undertook a number of roles, including journalist, media spokesman, technologist and product developer. In 1996, he led the team that launched one of the most successful internet service providers in Europe – Which? Online.

He is a former advisor to the UK Cabinet Office on communication strategy. As well as being a regular speaker at conferences around the world, he still broadcasts regularly on radio and television.

Acknowledgements

My thanks to Nikki Read, Giles Lewis, Debbie Robinson and Fiona Davis at *How To Books* for their faith and encouragement. To Gavin Campbell and Jeremy Nicholas for their assistance and advice. To Steve Webb, the best cameraman around. To Archana and Markus Schafer at The Knowledge Brokers, for giving me opportunities to use my skills in various countries. And to all TV and radio interviewers everywhere, who I hope will have an easier life as a result of this book.

Dedication

To Heather and Ellie, and to my dear Mum, June, who is much cleverer than she thinks she is.

Introduction

Andy Warhol was right. Everyone has their 15 minutes of fame these days. How you perform when your time comes can affect the reputation of your company, how you are seen professionally, and whether the call will ever come again.

Many people fear appearing on radio or television. They feel that they will be subjected to an interrogation, and made to reveal their deepest secrets. They think that every journalist is seeking ways to trap them in a corner and cause acute embarrassment.

Nothing could be further from the truth. The chances of most people being subjected to a withering attack by a media journalist are tiny. What journalists want is for you to tell your story, in a way that will inform, educate and entertain their listeners and viewers. The vast majority of journalists live in fear of unresponsive, inarticulate interviewees, since it makes their job much harder.

The idea of this guide is to make life easier for everyone involved in the media. If you are an interviewee, it will show you how to prepare, what to expect, and how to perform professionally. If you are a journalist, it will help to ensure that your interviewees will be a pleasure to talk to.

There is a lot of information here, but it is designed to be used at short notice. The chapters should be self-explanatory.

There is no need to read the book from cover to cover (but if you do, thank you), since you should be able to select those chapters that are relevant to your needs.

Everyone should read the first five chapters (Being Media-Ready, Your Core Message, Your Voice, Your Personal Appearance and Body Language). Then simply select the chapter or chapters that you need. Chapter 11 (Handling Questions) is a handy reminder for any type of interview. If you are dealing with a crisis, go straight to chapter 12 (Dealing with a Crisis).

The media works to very tight deadlines, and therefore you need to react quickly. If you are reading this in the green room, a few minutes before your appearance, just focus on chapter 2 (Your Core Message). And take a deep breath before you go in to the studio. Good luck.

How to use this book

As explained above, this book consists of general chapters, followed by chapters on each type of medium. Most importantly, there are five-minute guides and checklists to ensure that you have covered everything. You may find it useful to make copies of these on separate sheets for your own use, rather than scribble all over this delightful volume.

Five-minute guides

The idea of the five-minute guides is to act as a revision sheet of the key points in each chapter. They are not intended to be used alone, and you will need to have read the chapter first. It only takes a few minutes. These guides are most useful a few hours before an interview, when you still have time to correct any omissions in your preparation.

Checklists

The checklists are self-completion forms which will be specific to each interview. You should start to fill them in as soon as you can, even if you do not have all of the information available. When you have completed them, keep them with you until the interview is over. In some cases, you may be able to refer to them during the interview (but not on TV, please). However, their main use is as revision sheets in the few minutes before you 'go live'. Make full use of them – they will prove to be invaluable. You will find them in the relevant chapters, with more copies in the appendix.

1 · Being Media-Ready

A call from a reporter can come at any time of the day or night, any day of the year. Of course, sometimes you will be expecting it – for example, if you have been trying to generate publicity or your company has suffered a crisis. However, most of the time, the call will come out of the blue. You need to be ready.

The worst thing that you can do is to try to 'wing it', particularly if you are not used to being interviewed. The outcome could well be a disaster for your company, and worse, for you personally. Preparation is key to a successful media experience, and anyone who may talk to a reporter (that's *anyone*) should be media-ready.

Knowing your facts

You have been asked to do a media interview. Why? Because you are an expert, that's why. You know more about the topic under discussion than anyone else, or at least more than anyone else who is available at the time. You definitely know more than the audience, and probably more than the interviewer. I say 'probably' because specialist interviewers, such as business correspondents, develop a wide knowledge of their topic, and indeed thrive because of it. However, they won't flaunt their knowledge in front of you, so don't worry. You are the expert.

Knowing your business

You need to *sound* like an expert. You therefore need, at the very least, to be able to answer basic questions about your organisation. For example, if you represent a company, you should know the number of employees, locations, goods and services produced, and financial information such as the latest annual figures, as well as the company's plans for the future. Similarly, if you are speaking on behalf of a not-for-profit organisation, you should know the current activities, as well as details of recent successes and failures.

In short, you should know what you are talking about. The best way to do this is to have a 'backgrounder', which is a one-sheet summary of all of the above (see the end of this chapter for an example). You can prepare this yourself, or have it put together by someone with responsibility for communications. Most importantly, ensure that the details are checked by someone with appropriate knowledge (note: this is not always the managing director – often the most knowledgeable person is the company secretary).

Keep your backgrounder up to date by reviewing it every three months. If a major event occurs, such as a batch of redundancies, or a major new product, update it immediately. Make sure that every person who is likely to speak to the press has a copy, and keep a list of those people so that updates can be sent to everyone.

Consistency is just as important as accuracy. If one member of your organisation is giving out a different message to other spokespeople, that will become a story in itself.

Thinking like a journalist

With all types of communication, the key is to be able to understand the person that you are talking to, discover what they want, and supply it to them. Journalists are regarded by many people with suspicion, because they are seen as interrogators who will try to make you reveal information. While it is true that there are a few journalists who adopt this adversarial approach (you know who I mean), most journalists are just like you and I. They have a job to do, which is to fill a few column inches in a newspaper, or a 30-second report on the lunchtime news bulletin. They are often under pressure, harassed and desperate to finish a job almost before it is started.

The main motivation of a reporter is to do the job specified by their editor, as quickly and efficiently as possible. If you can help them to do this, you will find that the interview will go well, and you will become a trusted contact that they will return to again and again for expert comment.

A journalist will always be thinking, 'What will my audience be interested in?' You need to be thinking along the same lines. You need to find out as much as possible about the audience in advance of the interview so that you can tailor your responses accordingly. We'll be looking at ways of assessing the audience later in this guide.

There are several different types of journalist that you may encounter. Here are some examples.

The people's friend

If you find yourself on the morning sofa, you can expect a fairly easy time. However, if you aren't a regular viewer of this type of show, you may be surprised by some of the topics that are covered. If you are dealing with what (to you) appears to be a controversial area, be prepared for some very direct questions.

The breakfast interrogator
On a serious, news-heavy programme, you may encounter a serious seeker after truth who will give you a hard time. In practice, this is only likely if you are a politician or company director with embarrassing financial results. With other interviewees, at other times, the same tigerish journalist will turn out to be a pussy cat.

The local hero
On a regional news show, some of the journalists are 'wannabee' breakfast interrogators, so you may get the worst time of all. However, since your questioner will be inexperienced, you should be able to take control - at least you will if you take the advice in this book.

The drivetime dozer
A staple of local radio programming is the 'drivetime' show, which accompanies weary commuters on their way home. This is often a mixture of middle-of-the-road music and relaxed chatter. Often the home of experienced presenters, you are likely to get a long interview - perhaps up to ten minutes - without any tough questions at all. The important thing here is to have a core message that you keep repeating.

The jokey, blokey mate
There are many interviewers (of both sexes) who fit into this category. Indeed, some radio stations employ only this type of presenter. They will greet you like a long-lost friend, and refer to you by your first name or a nickname that they have

just invented. If this is not your sort of thing, you may have to grit your teeth, but the best advice is to relax and enjoy yourself.

The last worder
If you are interviewed by one of a pair of journalists, most likely on a breakfast or drivetime show, you may find that the other journalist is apparently not interested. Just when you think that your ordeal is over, they may lean towards you and say 'Could I just ask one more question before we finish?' If this happens, be on your guard, since the question will often be a tricky one. You can relax when you get back to the green room.

Why journalists are your friends

When you are being interviewed, your aim is to get your message across as succinctly as possible. The aim of the interviewer is to find out what you know, and encourage you to explain it as clearly as possible. Can you see a common interest here?

Rather than being wary of journalists, you should see them as willing partners in the business of message delivery. Almost everyone that you meet in the media will be friendly and helpful, provided that you are friendly and helpful to them. If you approach an interview with mistrust, trying to guard your 'secrets', not only will you not enjoy the experience, but you will make future interviews more difficult.

I'm not suggesting that you should invite every journalist that you meet round for dinner. However, treating them with courtesy, respect and general friendliness will pay dividends, and will guarantee that they are less combative.

If and when you do come up against an interviewer who spurns your chummy approach, there are other techniques that you will need to use, and we'll learn about those in a later chapter.

How to prepare

Since a reporter can call at any time, you need to be 'ever ready'. This does not mean that you have to be fully briefed about everything that your organisation does. You will have your own area of expertise, and that is what you should know inside out. If you are asked to comment about another topic, you need to know where to find the information at short notice, and who to speak to to find out more. Keep your backgrounder handy, maybe even on your wall.

What to do when a reporter calls

You may experience a variety of emotions when a call arrives from a journalist: panic, flattery, excitement or nervousness (probably a combination of all of these). If you respond immediately, any of these emotions will affect your response, causing you to say something that you may later regret. You need to buy yourself some time.

So, when a reporter calls, you need to find a way to get time to gather your thoughts. It really doesn't matter what excuse you use. You could say that you have a phone call on another line, that you have an urgent appointment, or even that you have to answer a call of nature. The reporter may object briefly, but they understand the rules of the game as well as you do.

Before you put down the phone, there is some vital information that you must acquire. You need to know the name of the journalist, where they are from, the subject of the enquiry, and their contact details. Don't ask what their deadline is, since the answer will almost always be 'five minutes ago'. Note down the details carefully, thank them for their call, and promise to call them back within 10 minutes.

Now, you have six or seven minutes to prepare yourself. Use the five-minute preparation guide and the backgrounder checklist (below) to make sure that you are ready. After about eight minutes, call them back. Don't be late.

If you have a company policy of channelling all media contacts through a communications department, make sure that you follow it. You may still end up doing the interview, but your internal experts will make sure that you are fully prepared.

Five-minute preparation checklist

Type of interview (live, pre-recorded, print)...........................

Medium (radio, TV, print, Internet)...

Media outlet (station or publication)......................................

Journalist ....

Contact number ....

Phone call or in person ....

Venue...

Time...

Arrangements (e.g. car pickup) ....

....

....

....

Message sheet completed? ....

Use the form above to ensure that you are aware of all necessary arrangements. In addition, you will need the Core Message Guide (see next chapter) to ensure that you have planned what you are going to say.

Backgrounder checklist

Organisation name ....

Main activities ....

....

....

When established..

Number of employees ....

Financial information (turnover etc)......................................

....

Locations..

....

Key people ....

....

Significant products/services ....

....

Recent announcements ....

2 · Your Core Message

Whenever we communicate, we convey a message. Otherwise the process is not communication, but simply making a noise. The art of good communication is to be able to convey the right message, in the right way, at the right time, to the right audience.

The essence of a message can always be distilled down to a core, being the precise detail that we wish to impart. The task of a media spokesperson (that's probably you) is to ensure that the soundbite that is used on news bulletins is the same as the core message.

Politics aside, one of the best core message communicators was the former UK Prime Minister, Margaret Thatcher. Whatever the situation, she made sure that she delivered her preferred soundbite. One of Britain's most skilled political journalists, Sir Robin Day, interviewed Lady Thatcher many times. When he retired and wrote his memoirs, a journalist enquired of him, 'Sir Robin, was there ever a question that you would have loved to have asked Margaret Thatcher, but never had the chance?' Sir Robin responded immediately, with a twinkle in his eye. 'Indeed there was,' he smiled. 'I always wanted to say to her, ''Mrs Thatcher, what is the answer to my first question?'''

The importance of a core message

When you sit down and plan what you want to say in an interview, you will probably come up with a list of points, all of which seem important. However, you need to focus on one, and one only.

So why can't you have a multi-point core message? Well, mainly it is because of the nature of the media. It is very likely that if one of your quotes is used during a broadcast news report, it will last for 10 seconds, at most. That means a maximum of about 30 words – hardly enough to list all the key points of your case. In addition, you need to think about your audience, who may be driving to work, making a family meal or glancing up from their newspaper at a TV report that has caught their eye. Unless you can deliver a brief and memorable message, all your efforts will have been wasted.

A core message is important because it will establish your credibility, show you to be in control, and ensure that people remember what you say.

Core message characteristics

In order to create your core message, you must know what you are looking for. Here is a checklist of the most important elements of a core message.

1. Identify the single most important idea
You will only be able to deliver one message. It therefore must be the most important thing that you want to communicate. In order to determine this, write down all the possible information that you think may be important. Imagine that you do not have time to mention all of it. Now discard the least important. Repeat the exercise until you only have one element left. That will be your core message.

Of course, whenever you try this, you will often find that you are left with two points that you cannot separate. If you can find a colleague (preferably someone who is not familiar with the story), ask their opinion. If you are all alone, there's an old journalistic trick that may work. Take a coin, and nominate one phrase as 'heads' and the other as 'tails'. Toss the coin. You will now have a winner. However, don't just leave it to chance. Think whether you are happy with the decision. If you would have preferred the other phrase to win, pick that one instead. It's as simple as that.

2. Keep it simple
It is almost impossible to convey a complex idea in a short interview, and almost all interviews are short. You therefore need to find a way to simplify your message (unless it is already simple).

A trick here is to imagine that you are speaking to a fairly bright 11-year-old child. (If you don't have one of your own I'm sure you will have met one, and this is only an exercise of the imagination.) Think how you would explain the idea to them using words that they would instantly understand. Don't use jargon, or industry-specific terms. Concentrate on the essence of the message.

3. Make it memorable
We are besieged with messages every day, through radio and TV, adverts, conversations and the like. Your job, when delivering your message on the media, is to make it something that people will remember.

There are several ways to create memorable messages, and we will look at some of them below (see 'The news hook'). For now, try to think of words and phrases that are a little unusual, or conjure up an image. If your message is 'seen' as a picture, even if you are on the radio, it will be much more memorable. Groucho Marx used to tell a story about the value of words. He asked a little boy whether he preferred radio or TV. 'Radio,' replied the boy at once, 'because the pictures are better.'

4. Make it relevant
As mentioned throughout this guide, understanding the audience is the key to good communication. The great communicators know this, and always start any consideration of a speech or media comment by thinking how the audience will react to it.

You have to put yourself in the shoes of your potential audience and think what they will find engaging. That's the hard part. All you have to do then is to deliver what they want to see or hear.

For example, if you are due to appear on a morning TV show, at around 11am, what sort of audience do you think might be watching? You have to be careful of stereotyping, but it is likely that the viewers will be a mixture of retired people and stay-at-home parents with small children. However, if you are on a late-night radio chat show, the listeners may well be insomniacs and stressed-out workers who have just arrived home after a very long day. Your message to these audiences will probably be very different, even if you are talking about the same product or service.

5. Stress the benefits
You also need to consider what benefit your message is offering the audience. Of course, this is one of the key elements of advertising, where agencies will often create a 'need', and then offer something to fulfil that need.

If you have prepared properly, and understand your audience, you should find it easy to mention a potential benefit. Remember that this may not be a benefit that they will enjoy directly. It may be something that will be of value to their family or friends, or to the community in general. Many people will respond to something that improves the overall quality of the environment, or the life of someone that they don't even know.

6. Ask yourself, 'So what?'

Imagine yourself hearing your own core message. If your immediate reaction is, 'So what?', then the message doesn't work. You need to be able to capture the value to your audience in whatever you say.

7. Be sincere

Over the years, I have met many company spokespeople who sound less than sincere about their products. I always ask them the same question: 'Is this a product you would use or buy?' They often shift a little from one foot to the other and say, 'Well, not really – but I'm not like our customers.'

In order to be believed, you have to be sincere. In order to be sincere, you have to really believe what you are saying. That is why it is very important for you, as a company spokesperson, to be involved in drafting the core message. It will be very difficult for you to recite words given to you by a PR person if you are not fully confident that they represent your opinion.

In the later chapter on crisis media management, I will be explaining how you must be honest and truthful at all times. If you ever bluff, someone will find out.

8. Putting it all together
In summary then, your core message needs to be simple, relevant, memorable, beneficial and, of course, true.

Equally as important as all of these characteristics is that you need to be clear about your message, and why it is important for you to be saying it at that moment. Don't worry, it isn't as hard as it sounds.

The news hook
When a reporter looks at the possibility of covering your story, and asking you to be interviewed, they will be looking for the story, or angle. They are not interested in facts, other than those which support the story. For this reason, it is important that you understand the concept of the 'news hook'.

When you look at newspapers, consider the headlines carefully. A lot of thought has been put into them, and they represent the news hook. Few people read every story in a newspaper, but skim through, glancing at the headlines until something catches their attention.

A good news hook will attract attention by having an element of originality, or setting up a question that can only be answered by reading the story.

How to define the message
Brevity is not only the soul of wit, it is also the essence of a good core message. When you have decided what your message is, try to reduce the number of words, and try to simplify the vocabulary. Never believe that you can make your message too simple.

Some of the best core messages are advertising slogans. Consider the simplicity of these: 'Just do it', 'Go to work on an egg', 'We try harder'. Every message is simple, memorable, and captures the essence of the product.

How to deliver the message

Regardless of the question, it is your job to deliver your core message in every interview. This does not mean that you should completely disregard the question, but it does mean that you should steer the answer toward your desired response.

Imagine that you are being interviewed on a serious, news-based morning radio programme. Your company has suffered poor financial results, which have just been announced. The interviewer fixes you with his gaze, and says, 'So, it looks very much as though your company is going down the tubes. Have you considered how much redundancy pay you are going to make available?' Now, you may be tempted into making a 'How dare you?' response, but of course, you are a media professional, so you respond thus: 'Let me clarify the position. We have suffered a dip in revenue, along with every other company in our sector. However, we are now starting to see an upturn, and *we have just won our biggest-ever contract.* Redundancies are not on the agenda.' The core message is in italics.

Of course, you need to beware of 'hostage to fortune' syndrome. Don't make your core message something that you may later regret.

Deliver your core message with confidence and clarity. Make an effort to slow down as you say it. You want to ensure that it is the message that is remembered.

Of course, you don't have to use exactly the same form of words every time. If you are repeating the message several times during an interview, you could vary the wording slightly, provided you do not alter the meaning.

The first and last time you use the message in an interview, stick to the original wording.

Stunning facts

As mentioned above, journalists are looking for much more than facts. They are looking for a story. The way in which you present facts can make the difference between being reported and being ignored.

If you are speaking on behalf of an aircraft manufacturer, you may well have a mass of facts about a new aircraft. Some of them may be quite astonishing (to you, at least), and you decide, correctly, to include them during your interview. Let's say that the wingspan of your new passenger plane is the largest of any commercial airliner, stretching to just over 80 metres. You say to the interviewer, 'Our new airliner is enormous, with a wingspan of 81.5 metres.' While true, that fact won't resonate with the audience, since most of them can't visualise what it means. However, if you say, 'The wings on our airliner are so large they would stretch from one penalty spot to the other on a football pitch,' the audience is stunned. People are imagining being at their local football ground and seeing your plane covering most of the playing area.

You should always try to link your facts to examples that will make them come alive. Once you have come up with a stunning fact, use it over and over again in interviews and publicity material, so that people will remember it.

You can always tell when a stunning fact has hit home. You will find it referred to in stories on air, in newspapers, and on the Internet. If you really hit the jackpot, you may even find it quoted back to you in conversation, although, alas, people probably won't know who coined the phrase.

Five-minute core message guide

If you have five minutes to prepare your core message, this is what you do.

1. List five important points about the interview topic. Keep each one brief – no more than 10 words.

2. On a separate sheet of paper, write down three sentences about your potential audience. Include characteristics like geographical region, age profile, gender profile, interests.

3. Look at your list of five points, and discard the two least important.

4. Compare the two lists. Determine which of your key points is most relevant to your audience.

5. Define your core message, and try it out on a few colleagues (ring them up if necessary!).

6. Practise using your core message until it is word perfect.

As a last-minute check, ask yourself the following questions.

- Does the message make sense?

- Is it the most important thing you want to say?

- Does it stand on its own, without further explanation?

- Is it as simple as it can be?

- Is it relevant to the audience?

- Is it of benefit to the audience?

If the answer to any of these questions is 'No', then run through the five-minute exercise again.

You have to be absolutely sure of your message before you attempt to deliver it.

Core message planner checklist

Message 1 ....
Keep? Y/N

Message 2 ....
Keep? Y/N

Message 3 ....
Keep? Y/N

Message 4 ....
Keep? Y/N

Message 5 ....
Keep? Y/N

Audience

Type of interview ....

Date .... Time ....

Interviewer ....

TV/radio station ....

Description of likely audience ....

....

....

....

....

Final core message ....

....

....

....

....

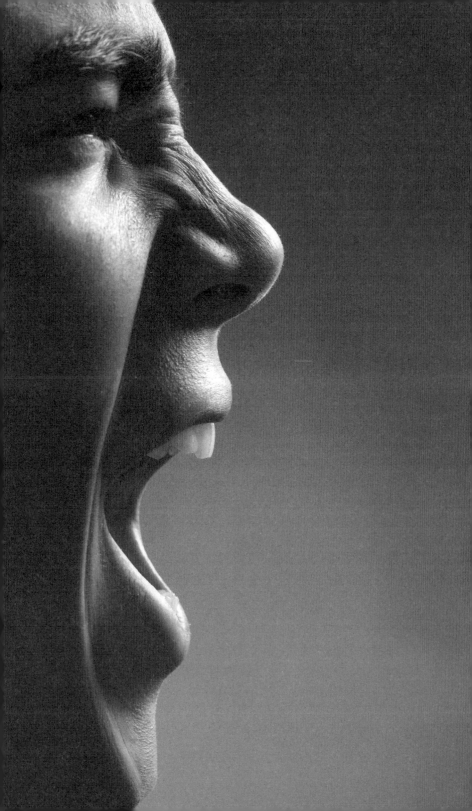

3 · Your Voice

Many people are known to us by the sound of their voices. Some of the great speakers came to prominence during the radio generation. But there is more to it than that. We all have the capacity to register subtle nuances in voices, without even realising that we are doing so. We can often tell when someone is lacking confidence, overstating their case, or even lying.

Your voice can become your defining characteristic. Indeed, the careers of many impressionists have been built on the fact that we often base our entire opinion of someone on how they sound. Think of Winston Churchill, Nelson Mandela or Margaret Thatcher, and you can instantly conjure up the sound of their voices. They are also wonderful examples of how their characters sound through, whether showing courage and determination (Churchill), quiet confidence and steadfastness (Mandela) or confidence and clear focus (Thatcher).

Your voice is unique to you, and I am not going to suggest that you should change it radically. The important thing is to sound confident, honest and clear. In this chapter, we will be considering some ways in which you can speak with style.

Breathing and relaxation
If you are not fully relaxed, your voice will give you away. Learning to breathe properly is one of the most important aspects of relaxation, leading to a confident performance.

When we talk normally, we only replace the air in the top part of our lungs. As we become more nervous, we tend to breathe more shallowly and more often, which can lead to hyperventilating if we start to panic. Sometimes, if you are really tense, you may find that you have been holding your breath without even realising it.

Conversely, if we breathe more deeply, exchanging larger volumes of air, more oxygen reaches the blood, and we breathe more slowly. Filling your lungs completely takes a bit of practice, but once you have learned the technique, it will become part of your everyday pattern of breathing.

The technique is known by various names such as 'diaphragm breathing' or 'belly breathing', but it all comes down to using your diaphragm to fill your lungs more deeply. Your diaphragm is a sheet of muscle below your ribcage, and you can use it by imagining that you are filling your lungs from the bottom upwards. As you breathe in, push your belly outwards, then expand your ribs, and finally your upper chest, right up to your neck. It may seem odd at first, but if you practice, initially for a few minutes each day, and then for longer periods, you will gradually become accustomed to it.

You should always breathe deeply before starting to speak.

Vocal exercises
You don't have to stand in front of a mirror and sing scales like Pavarotti. But since your voice is a crucial part of your media performance, you do need to keep it in good working order. Try to find a few minutes each day for these simple voice exercises and you will soon see the effect.

1. Stand with your feet slightly apart, with your arms hanging loosely at your sides. Roll your shoulders around and feel them relax. Take a few diaphragm breaths. Make a conscious effort to relax all over, from your head to your toes, by tensing each group of muscles and relaxing them as you slowly breathe out.

2. The next time you exhale, make a gentle 'ha' sound. Keep the sound going until you run out of breath. Breathe in deeply, using your diaphragm, and repeat the 'ha'. Do this five or six times.

3. The next time you breathe in, lift your shoulders up towards your ears. Keep them up and count silently to five. Exhale, and relax your shoulders. Repeat five times.

4. Now comes the tricky part. Combine the second and third exercises, by saying 'ha' as you relax your shoulders. By now, anyone in your vicinity will be looking at you in alarm. Ignore them. You will be much more relaxed than they are.

If you can find somewhere suitable, try to do a few of these exercises before any interview. You will find that you are not only more relaxed, but also more alert, because of the extra oxygen you are putting into your bloodstream. With your core message, relaxed manner, and sharp mind, you will be a match for any interviewer.

Speaking with clarity
In order to get your message across, you must speak as clearly as possible. Many speakers, particularly when they are nervous, tend to speak more quickly, making them harder to understand. You need to make a real effort to speak more

slowly – in fact, it is almost impossible to speak too slowly in an interview.

Using pauses is one of the most effective ways to improve communication. Not only does it help you to gather your thoughts, but it also helps your audience to digest and understand what you have said. It can be very difficult to get used to using pauses, since we all have set speaking patterns. It is well worth the effort, though. You can practise pausing by counting silently to five at the end of each phrase or sentence. The first time you try, it will seem like a lifetime, but persist until you are used to it. You will find it much easier to do if you talk to someone else, as they will be able to give you the feedback that it sounds just fine.

One of the best ways to improve your clarity is to change the pitch of your voice. We have all heard speakers who deliver in a monotone, causing most of their audience to doze off. You should aim at raising and lowering the pitch of your voice occasionally to maintain interest. Overall, try to lower your voice more than raising it, since this is easier on the ear of your listeners.

When you are using a microphone, the technician will adjust the output so that it sounds as clear as possible. Take your cue from your interviewer, and keep the same distance from the mike as they do. Some interviewees make the mistake of either leaning forward (which causes 'popping' sounds), or leaning back (so that the technician has to adjust the sound quickly). Instead, sit in a relaxed way, leaning slightly forward, and talk in your normal voice.

Accents and dialects

Some people worry about their accents when they are due to be interviewed. These days this is not a problem, since all types of accent are now common on both radio and TV. However, you do need to be aware of any local dialect words that may confuse a wider audience. A friend of mine, top professional speaker Kenny Harris, tells of the unusual way that certain Scottish folk sometimes respond. 'If you ask a Glaswegian a question, and he says "Aye, right," he means "No"' says Kenny. 'They're probably the only people who can put two positives together to make a negative.' All over the world, there are words and phrases that can puzzle your audience. As ever, the best advice is to keep it simple.

Taking care of your voice

Your voice is very important, and needs to be looked after. Prior to an interview, avoid straining your voice in any way, even by repeated rehearsals. You may be word perfect, but if your voice sounds croaky, that's what people will remember.

If you are a smoker, you won't want me telling you to give up. However, if you know that you have an interview looming, try to cut down just beforehand to give your lungs a rest. Alcohol and caffeine can also affect the voice, so take it easy there too.

If you find yourself hoarse, try tea with lemon, or room-temperature water with lime. Chilled water or water with ice is not a good idea, as the sudden change in temperature can give your voice a shock.

If you have a persistent voice problem, have it checked out to see whether anything needs to be done.

Five-minute voice preparation guide

- Run through your voice exercises.

- Don't over-rehearse.

- Limit alcohol, coffee and smoking.

- Take a deep breath before you speak.

- Slow down.

- Use pauses.

- Avoid dialect, but don't worry about your accent.

- Vary the pitch of your voice.

- If using a microphone, copy the interviewer.

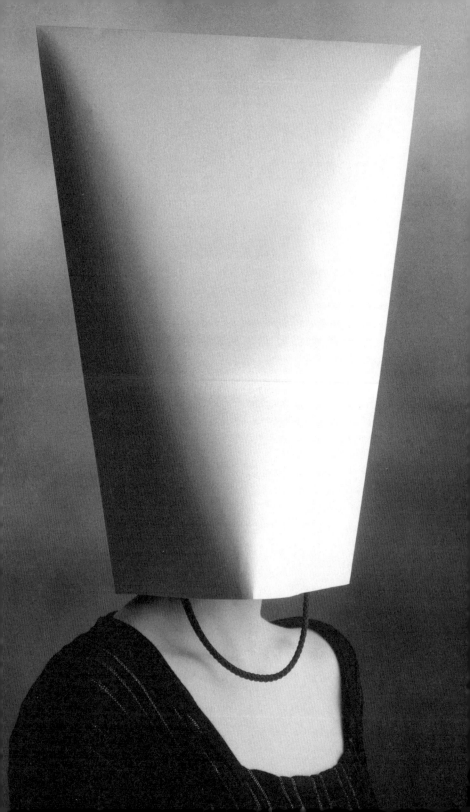

4 · Your Personal Appearance

When coaching executives in media skills, I often use an exercise to demonstrate how important image can be, particularly at times of crisis. Several years ago, following a tragic shipping accident with significant loss of life, the managing director of a shipping company agreed to give an interview to a TV news crew. I show a clip of the interview, and ask 'What message did that interview convey?' The response is always something like, 'He clearly wasn't too concerned about the victims, but more about the financial effect, or whether he might lose his job.'

I then play the clip again, with the picture turned off, so that we can hear only the words. This time, the impression is very different: 'What an excellent interview.' 'He said exactly the right things, and is clearly very concerned about the victims and their families.'

The importance of visual impact
So why is there such a difference? It is all down to visual impact. When I play the clip for the third time, I ask people to study the appearance of the managing director. They quickly realise that they have made a judgement because of the way that he looks. It happened that the accident occurred at the weekend, and the managing director had

been at a charity event, wearing a casual outfit and a rather natty trilby hat. He looked as though he had just been out enjoying himself, and the interview had been somewhat of an inconvenience. Even though he performed very professionally, and showed great concern, the overriding impression was the opposite.

How you dress, how you stand and how you move all work together to create an impression of whether you are sincere and trustworthy. This is particularly important where you have only a few seconds to make your point. If your appearance is wrong, there is no time to overcome the initial impression that you make, and you may be remembered for how you looked, rather than for what you said.

Being comfortable

In addition to how you are perceived by others, your appearance can affect how you feel. In order to deliver a confident performance, you need to feel good about yourself, and only you can be the judge of that. Even if others tell you that you look fine, you will know whether you are happy with your appearance.

Somewhat surprisingly, your appearance is important on radio too. For the reason just mentioned, if you are feeling good about yourself, you will perform better. Not only that, but the way that you look will affect how radio interviewers treat you. If you are speaking on behalf of a professional body, such as a group of lawyers, you will not be taken so seriously if you arrive at the studios wearing jeans and a t-shirt. On the other hand, if you are an eco-warrior, a three-piece pinstripe suit may be inappropriate.

Of course, some people use their appearance to create the impression that they are different from their peers. Derek Hatton, when he was deputy leader of Liverpool City Council, used to wear sharp suits that set him apart from his left-wing colleagues. Regardless of his motivation, his appearance certainly got him noticed, and probably stirred up more feeling (both pro- and anti-) about him than anything that he said.

Projecting confidence

It is crucial that you look and feel confident. Although you may have a good story to tell, your appearance may be giving a difference message. In the next chapter, we'll look at how your body language can affect how you are perceived. As far as your appearance is concerned, I'm not going to go into great detail here, but would suggest that if you are concerned about how you look, you should consider working with an expert in personal branding.

Here are some basic elements about your personal appearance that you should consider:

Clothes. Wear something comfortable and fashionable. Don't even think about wearing something new for the first time. You may be under hot lights for quite a time, and the last thing you want is to have something constricting and uncomfortable. Brand-new shoes could be a nightmare, particularly if you have to walk along seemingly endless corridors to reach your TV studio.

Hair. Keep it neat and tidy. If you are interviewed on location, where it may be windy, bear that in mind. If you are prone to dandruff, find a shampoo that clears it up, since it will be very visible on TV, especially if you are wearing a dark suit. Men who are bald or balding will need makeup (see below).

Jewellery. Keep it subtle. Anything that catches the light will be a distraction. Dangly ear-rings or flashy watches will also become the focus of attention, and detract from your message (unless you are a jeweller).

Make-up. Again, keep it subtle. Both men and women will need make-up for television, because of the effect that cameras and studio lights can have. The cameras magnify any imperfections, and the lights tend to throw more pronounced shadows on your face. Unless you are wearing make-up suited to TV studios, you will look quite unwell. If you are not a regular TV performer, you should allow the make-up artists to do their work. Men need not be embarrassed, even if they forget to take off their make-up after leaving the studio; everyone will say to you, 'You do look well – have you been on holiday?'

Glasses. If you wear glasses only for reading, then don't wear them on television, other than to refer to any notes (hopefully you won't need to). Avoid frames that are too heavy, or lenses that reflect the light. TV presenters wear glasses with a special non-reflective coating. This may be worth considering if you are planning to do a lot of TV work. Tinted glasses or sunglasses are not usually appropriate unless you have an eye condition, or you are a hip-hop diva being interviewed on MTV.

Tips for television
Here are a few more pointers to think about for TV appearances:

Hair is important and so is your top/blouse/shirt. You can't really see anything else, so don't spend hours agonising over trousers and shoes.

Wear something neutral. You want people to listen to you, not be amazed at your outfit. Don't wear a white shirt. The camera doesn't like it, as it's too bright under the lights. Don't wear small checks as they strobe on camera.

Wear a belt. You'll be given a microphone to wear, with a battery pack attached. You'll need to clip this onto your belt. If you haven't got a belt, you can tuck the pack in your pocket. Wear a top that will be easy to clip a microphone onto. A button-up shirt or v-neck top is ideal. A polo neck is a nightmare.

Learn how to put your own mike on unless you want a sound technician putting their hand up your back. Use gravity, as it's easier to drop the pack down, than thread the mike up.

What to avoid
Here's a checklist of what to avoid:

Avoid rushing. If you know you are being interviewed first thing in the morning, plan your outfit the day before, and have it ready. Some early morning interviews may require a pickup at some unearthly hour (I speak from experience here). If you want to stay friends with your partner, put your clothes and accessories in a spare room, and sneak out quietly. The alternative (and here I speak from experience again) is to stumble around and try to get dressed in the dark. This is not a good idea for many reasons.

Avoid new clothes. As mentioned above, a media interview is not the time to try out a new outfit. If you do want to wear something new, make sure that you buy the clothes some time in advance, and wear them a couple of times before the big day (you can get them cleaned, of course).

Avoid white. White does not look good on television, as the camera will 'balance' for its brightness. This will make you and the rest of your outfit fade into the background. If the studio is using a 'blue screen', then they will also tell you to avoid blue, or part of you will definitely be part of the background.

Avoid anything distracting. Ask someone to check whether any part of your outfit is causing a distraction. It may not be easy for you to tell, as you may be used to your flashing medallion.

Avoid fidgeting. If you regularly fiddle with a ring or a bracelet, try to stop yourself for the duration of the interview. Again, you may need to ask someone for advice, since you may not be aware that you are fidgeting. The easiest way to stop is to clasp your hands together (not too hard!) in your lap.

Five-minute appearance guide

Before you head off for that interview, take a few minutes to run through this quick checklist:

- Am I dressed comfortably?

- Do I look the part?

- Is my outfit 'TV friendly'?

- Is my outfit 'microphone friendly'?

- Is there anything that will take attention away from my words?

- If I am doing several interviews in a day, do I need a change of clothes?

- Are my shoes clean?

- Any missing buttons or loose threads?

- Do I need to take any pens out of my pockets?

- Do I need a coat/umbrella for outside interviews?

- Is my mobile phone in my pocket? (Remember to turn it off before the interview.)

5 · Body Language

These days, we all know something about body language. Whether we learnt it from author and person-watcher Desmond Morris, or by becoming an NLP (Neuro-Linguistic Programming) practitioner, we are all aware that our bodies can give away things that we aren't saying. There can even be a conflict between the way that we present ourselves and what we say. This chapter is not intended to be a complete course in body language, but aims to provide you with some tips and pointers that you can use to improve your communication on the media.

There is an oft-quoted statistic that 55 per cent of the impression we create is related to body language, 38 per cent to the way we speak, and 7 per cent to the words themselves. I must admit that I find these figures somewhat unhelpful, and I suspect that they apply in only very limited circumstances. If these percentages were usually true, we should be able to learn to communicate in a foreign country by copying the way that people move and use their voices. I have always found it more effective to learn the vocabulary. However, this is not the place for debate. There is no doubt that body language is extremely important, so let us consider how it can be used.

Posture

When John F Kennedy won the US presidential election over Richard Nixon in 1960, he was keen to portray a healthy, young image. Both the election debates and the set-piece speeches highlighted a difference in the way the candidates were perceived. JFK always stood upright, and looked relaxed and tanned (it is said that he wore layers of thermal underwear so that he never had to wear a coat except in the coldest weather). Nixon, in contrast, adopted a hunched stance, often looking uncomfortable. JFK won, but Nixon had learnt his lesson, and in 1968, having updated both his wardrobe and his posture, was elected president. The impact of television on political careers had begun. If this seems an over-simplification, it probably is, but if you have the chance to watch archive footage of those presidential debates, you can see the contrast.

Your posture can make you appear relaxed and interested, or ill at ease and hostile. Very often, TV interviews will be conducted across a desk. This immediately places a barrier between you and the interviewer, which makes it more difficult to have a friendly interaction.

If you are leaning back in your chair, arms folded and looking down your nose at your interviewer, it is pretty obvious how you feel. On the other hand, if you are leaning forward, hands clasped together on the desk in front of you, listening intently, you create a completely different image.

Whatever you feel about the questions being asked, your posture should indicate interest, since you want your response to be listened to. Polite attention is the image you should aim for.

If you are interviewed in the open air, you will usually be standing up. In order to adopt a confident stance, stand with your feet a few inches apart. Just before the interview starts, pivot on the balls of your feet and bring your heels together. You will find that your stance subtly changes, as your back straightens, your shoulders widen, and your chin moves up. You will look and feel more confident, and viewers will notice.

Being neutral

Your interviewer will probably act as a 'devil's advocate', and ask questions that sound as though they oppose your position. They may even adopt a closed or aggressive posture, in order to reinforce their points.

Just as you should not react verbally, you should not indicate non-verbal conflict either. The interviewer is simply doing their job, by asking questions that the viewers would ask. There is no need to react by folding your arms, crossing your legs, or turning away.

Your stance and gestures should be neutral, conveying neither aggression nor friendship. Treat the interviewer with respect in a professional manner.

Being open and honest

The way that you gesture can convey openness and honesty. Unbuttoning your jacket, or even removing it, can indicate that you are ready to get down to business.

Nodding in agreement is a good idea, and something that the producer will often use as a reaction shot. If you overdo the nodding, however, it looks automatic, and can convey that you have lost interest, but are trying to feign it.

Hands

Once, TV interviewees were told to keep their hands still. For some people (me included) this makes it more difficult to communicate, since our hand gestures are linked closely to our speech.

There is no need to sit on your hands when you appear on TV. Natural hand gestures are fine, provided you remember a few guidelines. Many of us were told as children that it is rude to point. That rule still applies. Pointing at an interviewer or debating opponent is an aggressive gesture, as is making a chopping motion with one hand into the other palm. A closed fist is a very clear symbol of your discontent.

On TV, keep your hand gestures within the frame formed by your shoulders, sides and waist; otherwise they may disappear outside the picture, which looks very odd. Avoid touching your face or hair. Keep your palms upward to convey openness. A gesture which many politicians are taught to use is the 'steeple', with the fingers pointing upwards, fingertips together and palms apart. It conveys confidence, but don't overdo it, or it will look false.

Eyes

Eye contact is very important. You should try to make eye contact with your interviewer the whole time. If you find this a little disconcerting, you can try focusing on the tip of their nose, or just above their eyebrows. No one will notice.

Don't be too put off if your interviewer seems distracted, and looks away while you are answering. It is likely that they will be listening to the voice of their producer (and possibly several other advisors) in their earpiece. It's nothing personal.

If you are taking part in a down-the-line interview (see the chapter on television skills), then eye contact is critical. However, there is no one to look at, simply a camera lens. Whether you find this easier or more difficult is a matter of personal taste, but it is a media skill that you need to master.

Most importantly, keep your gaze upward. Looking down can indicate uncertainty, or a lack of self-esteem. My father, an engineer, used to tell an appropriate one-liner: 'How can you tell an extroverted engineer from an introverted engineer?' 'An extroverted engineer looks at your shoes.'

Walking and talking

Walking and talking simultaneously doesn't sound all that difficult, does it? When you add the fact that you are being interviewed, and that you need to follow a camera crew fairly closely, it can become tricky.

Do you look where you are going, or look at the interviewer? I suggest a combination of both, though your main focus, as ever, is the person you are talking to. Take your lead from the people around you, and you will be fine.

I was once interviewed at Goonhilly Down in Cornwall, on a very windy day. The combination of a force eight gale, having to step over cables, avoiding being struck by large moving radio dish receivers, and having to talk intelligently to an interviewer was quite an experience.

Thankfully, 'walkie-talkie' interviews are quite rare, and should you ever find yourself having to perform in one, you can console yourself with the fact that the camera operator is in front of you, and walking backwards, so they will definitely encounter any hazards first!

Five-minute body language guide

■ Lean forward and look interested.

■ Make a conscious effort to relax.

■ Stand with your weight on the balls of your feet, not your heels.

■ Look up rather than down.

■ Don't fidget or fiddle with your hair.

■ Smile slightly.

■ Be aware of the people around you, and 'include' them.

■ Show your passion.

6 · Talking to Print Journalists

It is quite likely that your first encounter with a journalist will be a reporter from the local paper. You may well have passed this hurdle already, but similar rules apply, whether you are talking to the young and keen reporter from the local *Echo* to the business correspondent from *The Times*.

By the way, don't dismiss local papers as something to move upwards from. They have a very loyal and strong readership, and often franchise stories around their 'stable' of papers. If you tell a good story to a local reporter, it can appear in 20 or more papers over a wide area, and may then be sold on to the national press.

In addition, radio and TV researchers scan newspapers for stories that they can broadcast. Getting print coverage should be a very important part of your media strategy. In this chapter, we will consider straightforward steps to ensure that you receive the best possible publicity.

Doing your research
Many print publications are aimed at a small target market, which may be a local area, particular profession or special interest. In order to make sure that your story is printed, you

need to do a little research, so that you can provide an angle which will appeal to the readership.

With local papers, of course, the angle is clear. The trick is to make the local link as obvious as possible. Don't worry about it appearing to be too contrived. As long as the name of the town or village appears in the opening line, the story will be of interest. Have a look at your own local papers to get an idea of how they work. It will be useful to note which reporters write each story, since there may be someone with a particular interest in your type of news. If so, try to speak to them directly.

Also consider whether your story is 'news' or 'features'. News stories are more immediate, and include items such as a new product or service, a reaction to another story, or a protest. They tend to appear on the first few pages (or the back for sports stories), and often include arresting images. Features are lengthier, often with 'human interest', and usually written some time before publication. They provide the opportunity for a more in-depth story.

The letters to the editor may also be a way to get your story into print. They can benefit you in a couple of ways. Firstly, they provide a direct route to an audience, and usually appear exactly as you have written them, giving you the chance to make your points clearly and thoroughly. Secondly, they may prompt a call from a reporter if they think that the story is newsworthy (or 'featureworthy'). If you decide to take this route, remember that a brief letter is more likely to be published in full, and you shouldn't try a 'hard sell', otherwise your words won't appear at all. Most papers now accept letters by email, so you don't even have to buy a stamp.

Writing a column

If you really want to make a name for yourself, and have an hour to spare each week, offer to write a column (this may be known as an 'opinion piece' or 'op-ed' – short for 'opposite the editorial page'). If you have information that is of special interest to the readers, approach the editor of a journal and make the offer. Explain your expertise, and include an example of your writing. Don't expect to get paid, though. Budgets are very tight, and your payback will be the regular publicity that you receive, and contact details at the end of your piece. Be aware that if you make a commitment to a regular column, you will be facing a regular deadline, just like a real journalist. If you are new to this type of thing, find a publication that appears monthly, or even better, quarterly, so that you don't over-commit yourself.

For special interest publications, you also need to have an angle, which again should be obvious. If you are struggling to find the connection between your story and the publication, then you probably shouldn't pursue it. You can always resort to the all-purpose statement 'Many of my friends are (fill in name of special interest here), and they tell me that one of the most important issues facing them today is ...'

The first contact

Unless a crisis has occurred, it is unlikely that a reporter will call you. It is more likely that you, or your PR company, will have issued a press release or statement, which has been deemed to be of interest.

Be prepared by having any information that you sent out handy, as well as supporting material to back up your case. If you receive a direct call unexpectedly, you should always buy yourself a little time for thought (see chapter 1: Being

Media-Ready). Most importantly, find out who the journalist is, and why they are calling. It may be that they have a very different view of the story, or may be contacting you as an expert to discuss another story altogether.

One of the most important things to find out is whether the journalist is staff or freelance, since they are subject to different pressures, and often require information presented in a different way. Staff journalists ('staffers') work for one publication and will tend to be either young, keen reporters climbing the career ladder, or mature editors and sub-editors who like the security of a regular pay packet. They are more likely to have time to chat to you, attend press events and 'do lunch'. For your part, you should know something about their publication before talking to them.

Freelancers, on the other hand, write for a range of publications, and are more likely to be under pressure, since they are paid by the word. Always ask a freelancer where the article will appear, and if they are working on anything else that you can help them with. Once you become a valued contact for a freelance journalist, they will call you regularly.

Journalists are almost always working to tight deadlines, and they may want to get as much information from you as they can as quickly as possible. However, if they decide to turn the story into a feature, they will often offer to meet you face to face, probably with a photographer in tow.

Telephone interviews
Print journalists gather most of their information over the telephone. Although many of them write shorthand, the skill is declining, and you are more likely to be asked if you are happy for the call to be recorded. There is nothing sinister

about this, and it makes sense to agree. Remember, though, that there is no such thing as 'off the record', particularly if your answers have been permanently saved. Stick to the facts, and don't speculate or exaggerate. In other words, treat it exactly as you would if it was a radio interview (see the next chapter for more detail).

You should also make a note of the questions that you were asked, and the responses that you gave. It is unusual to have to challenge a story, but if you do, you will need to have some evidence. There is a much more important reason for keeping notes, though, and that is to refer back to if the reporter calls again, possibly to clarify a point, or to find out more information. If a colleague takes the call instead of you, it will be difficult for them to know what was said.

The great advantage of telephone interviews is that you are able to have all of your prompt sheets in front of you, so that you can deliver your core message, make all of your points, and deal with any awkward questions with consummate ease. At least, you will if you are media-ready!

Face-to-face interviews
If a journalist makes an appointment to meet you to discuss a story, it will often be because a photograph is required. You might be asked to suggest a location that would provide a suitable backdrop for a picture to accompany your story. It is more likely, however, that the journalist will already have a venue in mind, so be prepared to go with their idea. You might wish to refer back to chapter 4 (Your Personal Appearance) before going in front of the lens.

Of course, a face-to-face interview means that you won't be able to refer to notes, so you will need to prepare more carefully. It would also be impolite, and impractical, for you to be making notes during the interview, so you should find time as quickly as possible afterwards to jot down your impressions.

Because journalists are busy people (I know, you are too, but we're talking about getting good press coverage here), you should make sure that you are not late for your meeting. Unfortunately, journalists may be late, or even have to cancel, if another story breaks or over-runs. If this happens – and it will from time to time – don't get angry. It's the way the media works. When you get back to base, contact the journalist and offer them another appointment.

Supplying quotes

Quotes are always valuable to print journalists, and the more snappy and memorable, the better. You should prepare and practise your quotes before using them in conversation. The reporter will know that you didn't just make them up, but that doesn't matter, since what they are looking for is something to add life to the story, and that is what you are providing. Keeping your quotes short and to the point does require some work. As Mark Twain once said in a note attached to a letter to a friend, 'Sorry about the long letter, I didn't have time to write a short one.'

Case studies are also very popular with print journalists, since they can include direct quotes from 'real people'. It is quite in order for you to supply details of people that are available for interview, and have personal experience of whatever the story relates to. It is extremely time-consuming for journalists to find case studies, and they will be extremely grateful if you can do the work for them. Any case studies that you supply will almost certainly be sympathetic to your viewpoint, so the journalist may also try to find other people for a more balanced view. If you are feeling brave enough, you might supply those contacts too, but it is not your responsibility.

After the interview

When the interview is over, thank the journalist, make sure you have their contact details, and check when the piece is due to appear. If you are lucky, they may offer to send you the publication with your story in it. This is a very rare event. You will almost certainly have to seek it out yourself. If it is a magazine, you may have to wait several months before the article appears.

If you have promised to provide some more details, make sure that you do. Immediately after the interview, make a note of everything that you have promised to do, and make sure that you deliver. You will become exactly the kind of contact that journalists love.

There is some debate about whether you should contact a journalist to thank them after you have read the piece. In my experience, this alerts journalists to the fact that their article may not have been as 'balanced' as they intended. I would advise saying nothing, but if you must get in touch, you probably won't do much harm. If you really want to upset a journalist, keep calling pre-publication to ask how things are going, and whether you can offer any more information. As mentioned, journalists are very busy, and once they have finished a story and moved on, they do not want to be pestered by you. They will call you if they need something.

Five-minute print interview guide

- Supply a story, not information.

- Stick to the facts.

- Find out something about the publication, and tailor your message.

- Prepare quotes in advance, and use them appropriately.

- Be honest.

- Be concise.

- Ensure that you deliver any follow-up material promptly.

- Look for other opportunities – features, letters, opinion pieces.

- Help journalists do their job, and they will help you.

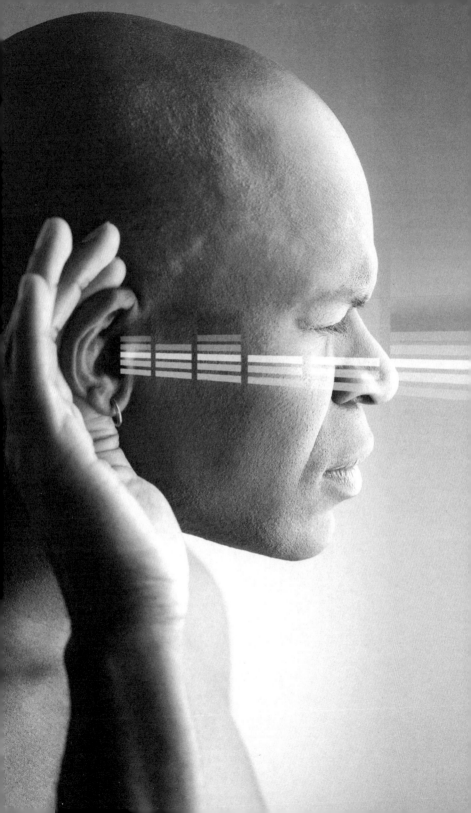

7 · Appearing on Radio

Radio, and in particular local radio, is probably the most effective way to reach an audience. More people listen to the radio than watch television, and much of the programming is factual, which means that radio stations are always on the lookout for guests.

The benefits of radio

You should never pass over the opportunity to appear on radio. You may never be asked again. If you accept and perform well (as you will, having read this book), you will be asked back time and again. Many interviews are pre-recorded, and can be done over the telephone. Even live interviews can be completed from the comfort of your own home. I have lost count of the number of radio interviews that I have done early in the morning, wearing a dressing gown and holding a mug of tea (most of them from home, too!).

Radio also allows you more opportunity to sound professional and well-informed, since you will often have your notes in front of you as you speak. The only time that this may not work is in a live studio interview, but even then you may be able to manage a sneaky glance at a prompt sheet. Whatever type of radio interview you do (in-studio, on location, pre-recorded), make sure that you get your core message in early. Repeat it at the end, and if possible say it in the middle too. That's what you're there for.

Using humour

Don't imagine that you always have to be deadly serious on radio (or on TV for that matter). OK, there are some subjects, such as disasters or death, where humour would not be an appropriate emotion. More often than not, it will be possible to inject a light-hearted note into a story, which will also serve to make it more interesting. It is a well-known tactic among professional speakers (of whom I am one) to deliver a serious point on the back of a laugh. It hits home much more effectively.

Knowing your stations

It is always a good idea to get a 'feel' for a radio station – and ideally the show itself – before you appear on it. Aim to listen to the station the day before you are due to appear, or at least a few hours before if you don't have much notice.

You will find that all radio stations have their own characteristics, which relate to the type of audience they serve. In the UK, BBC Radio 4 has a serious, authoritative tone, typified by presenters such as Nick Clarke. BBC Radio 5 Live has a more chatty style, with lots of listener involvement. Adrian Chiles embodies their style. Talk Sport is a 'blokey' station, where ex-footballer Alvin Martin and seasoned radio pro Mike Dicken appear.

You might be called to speak on any or all of these stations in the same day, and knowing their style will help you to delight their respective audiences.

Who does what in radio

Radio tends to have lower staffing levels than TV, as automation continues its advance across the media. Many radio stations now have more staff in their marketing departments than in their programming ones, so multi-skilling is also on the increase. Some radio stations now have no human intervention at all for many hours, relying instead on a digital jukebox to deliver music, jingles and programme trailers, with an hourly break for a real person, somewhere in the ether, to deliver a news bulletin.

However, on most radio stations, you will still find the following:

Presenter

This is the person who talks direct to the public, and who will probably conduct your interview, whether live in the studio or over the phone. They are often employed because of the quality of their voices, and their expertise in handling studio guests, opinionated phone-in callers and demanding producers all at the same time. They are not always beacons of sartorial elegance. I once did a serious interview on a well-known national radio station with a presenter who was wearing only a pair of swimming trunks and a Viking helmet. I never found out why. These days, with many studios being monitored by webcams, you are less likely to be confronted with such a spectacle.

Producer

The producer sits in the control room and ensures that everything runs smoothly, supplying information to the presenter through headphones. They carry out the decisions of the editor, and act as a link between the presenter and the in-house staff.

Technical operator (tech op)

The tech op is in charge of the technical elements of the studio, setting up adverts, station identifiers and external guests and correspondents. If you are doing a remote interview, you will probably talk to the tech op about the final arrangements, such as whether you can hear and be heard, and when you will be going live on air.

Researcher
You will probably have most contact with the researcher. They tend to contact guests, make arrangements for them to be interviewed, greet them on arrival and (if you are lucky) make the coffee. They are junior in the hierarchy, and usually very keen to move on in their career. Be nice to them. One day, they may be presenters, and they will remember you.

Editor
The editor is in overall charge. As a guest, it is unlikely that you will have much contact with them. If a big news story suddenly breaks, the editor will decide how to alter the show. If this means that your item is dropped, that's something you have to accept. If you become a regular radio interviewee, you will find that the editor's decisions are not always in your favour.

On the way to the studio
If you are travelling by train, cab or chauffeured car (if you are on a national radio station), use the time to good effect by reminding yourself of your core message, any other points, and topics that you need to avoid. If you are driving, rehearse some sample answers out loud.

If you are lucky enough to have a car sent to pick you up, make sure that you have contact details for the studio, and call them if the car does not arrive on time. They will be able to check whether the car is late, or lost.

If you chat to the driver on the way, be aware that your conversation may be passed on to someone at the studio. Although drivers usually work for a hire company, and not the radio station, they can be rewarded for passing on snippets of information, which later crop up in the interview. There's no need to be unduly wary, but it's best to keep your chat on a superficial level.

Make sure that you arrive in plenty of time, as you don't want to be flustered on air. Identify yourself at reception and wait to be collected, usually by a researcher. Again, if no one arrives after a few minutes, just check that you haven't been forgotten.

While you wait

When you are taken from reception towards the studio, you will probably be taken to the 'green room', which is never green, and usually not a room either. It is simply a term for the waiting area, and may be a sofa in the general office or a small room with a few chairs. There may be other guests waiting too. Probably the most useful thing to do is to listen to the output of the station. You will probably hear your interview being trailed ('... and after the news, we'll be speaking to Alan Stevens, a media expert ...'), and will have a chance to hear the previous speakers. It is always useful to 'back refer' during an interview, possibly to comments by a phone-in caller, or to someone with a different point of view about your subject. If you hear something that might be useful to refer to, make a note of it.

You may be taken directly to the studio, or into the control room, which is adjacent and has a soundproof window into the studio itself. Don't attempt to engage any of the control room staff in conversation unless they speak to you. They aren't being rude, just concentrating on their jobs.

In the studio

The first time that you enter a radio studio, you will probably find it much smaller than you expect. You will be taken into the radio studio just before your interview, and shown where to sit. There will be a microphone on the table, and a set of headphones (often called 'cans'). There is no need to put on the headphones unless you are directed to do so, since the interviewer is probably sitting just across the desk. They will be wearing headphones so that the producer and tech op can speak to them. Even if you put the headphones on, you won't hear the people in the control room.

If you are asked to put headphones on, it will be to hear someone from a remote location, or to listen to a recording. You probably won't be told, but there is a volume control at the end of the headphone lead, sometimes hidden just under the desk. Adjust the volume to suit yourself. You will also see a button on the desk in front of you marked 'cough' or 'PTM' (push to mute). Holding down the button turns your microphone off, should you need to clear your throat.

When the red light is on, the studio is 'live', and anything you say may be picked up by the microphones. Try to avoid rustling papers, swinging to and fro in your squeaky chair, or making any whispered asides. You may see various characters – news readers, sports correspondents and the like – entering and leaving the studio while the red light is shining. They (usually) know how to keep quiet. You should follow the instructions of whoever escorts you in and out.

Many radio studios have TV monitors tuned to news stations or information services. They are there to help the presenter keep up-to-date with breaking news. Try to ignore them. I remember being in a studio with another guest who was so mesmerised by a football match on one of the screens that he didn't hear his introduction, and was completely confused as he tried to answer the first half-heard question.

Other types of radio interview
Pre-recorded
Pre-recorded interviews are used for one of two purposes: to play in full, giving the presenter time to take a break, and to edit for clips to be used in trailers and news bulletins.

Interviews played in full – The first type, where both the questions and your answers are recorded for later broadcast, can be disconcerting. It may be that the interview is recorded on one day, and broadcast the next. It may be recorded for playback in the middle of the night. You should always ask when it is due to be broadcast, and then imagine that you are 'live' at that time. Let me explain what I mean. You may be asked to record an interview at 4pm on Tuesday, for broadcast at 7am on Wednesday. The interview may start with a cheery, 'Good morning' from the presenter. You need to respond as though it really is Wednesday morning, since when it is broadcast, the listeners will often have no idea that it is a recording, and will imagine that you are in the studio. It is only a slight subterfuge, but you need to play along with it. It may be easier for you to avoid all references to day or time, and simply say, 'Hello'.

Interviews for clips – The second type will probably be conducted by someone other than the presenter. They will have a list of questions, but not necessarily any interest in your responses. The whole process is not a discussion, simply a list of prompts to encourage you to make your points. You need to remember that the questions will not be broadcast, so you have to repeat them in your response, in order for the clip to make sense. If you are asked, 'How will you react to the workers' demands for higher pay?', it will not be helpful to respond, 'We're not going to budge on that issue.' Instead, you need to say something like, 'In response to demands for higher pay, our stance is to stick with our current offer.' In this type of interview, it is up to you to inject interest and emotion, since your questioner may not help you at all. On the positive side, if you deliver your core message in a punchy and memorable way, it will almost certainly be the clip that is used.

In all types of pre-recorded interviews, you need to be at your best at all times. You have no control over which clips will be broadcast, so you need to be sure that every answer is on the money.

Telephone interviews
Phone interviews are popular because they save on transport costs and can be set up at short notice. The great advantage for you is that you can use your pre-prepared notes to help you respond. The potential drawback is the quality of the telephone line, particularly if you are on a mobile phone. If you are asked to do a telephone interview, try to ensure that you have a good-quality connection, or you may find the interview suddenly terminated.

The process usually works like this. Firstly, you, or your communications department, will receive a call from a researcher asking if you are available for interview at a certain time. When agreement is reached, you should arrange to be somewhere that you won't be interrupted (put a sign on the door if necessary) and be available at least five minutes before the time agreed. You will receive a call from the studio, who will check that the line sounds fine, and that you can hear them and they can hear you. They will then switch the connection so that you hear the studio output, when you may hear your interview trailed ('... and coming up next, we'll be speaking to ...'). That's the time to get a few deep breaths in. You will probably hear a cue ('with you in 10 seconds'), and then the interview will start. When it is over, the tech op will cut in and thank you, at which point you can put down the phone and breathe a sigh of relief, before jotting down your notes.

Live on location
Radio interviews are usually conducted from the comfort of the studio, but if you are involved in sport or some other outdoor activity, you may find yourself in front of a microphone as soon as you finish your event. These interviews are usually fairly undemanding, with the first question often being, 'How do you feel?', so they don't require much preparation. As long as you avoid obscenities, and say what you are thinking, you will be fine. One exception to this rule, of course, is if you are a football manager discussing the performance of a referee. In that circumstance, 'no comment' may be the best option.

Occasionally, radio stations will set up a 'studio' in a remote location – for example, during the 2005 UK general election, BBC Radio 5 Live set up camp in a 'typical family home', which they called 'the house of commoners'. After a day or two, the occupants were so used to the microphones that they sounded like professional presenters. That's probably why radio stations don't do that very often.

Phone-ins and panel discussions
You may well be asked to participate in a phone-in about a controversial or topical issue. This will normally require you to

be in a studio, sometimes with just a presenter, sometimes with another expert.

Phone-ins give you the opportunity to talk for extended periods, and may require you to be on air for up to an hour. The drawback is that you won't always know what questions to expect. The discussion will be moderated by the presenter, who will control which callers come on air.

The presenter has a computer monitor on their desk, on which appear brief details of each caller, such as name and location, and what they want to discuss. Most presenters will offer you the chance to pick who to talk to, although if callers are few, they will select the one who has been waiting longest. If a caller is abusive, or uses obscenities, they can be cut off before their words are broadcast, since there is a broadcast delay of around seven seconds which allows them to be silenced.

Phone-ins are often prefaced by, or made part of, a panel discussion, where several experts air their views. If you take part in such a debate, be careful not to interrupt, and raise your hand to indicate to the presenter that you would like to speak. Always be respectful of your fellow panellists. Your case will sound more powerful if you stay calm.

After the interview

You may not be able to thank the presenter, as they will often still be on air as you leave the studio. A nod and a smile will suffice.

Always leave your contact details at the studio. Someone who heard your interview may call in and ask for your details. It could be a potential customer.

As soon as you can, think about how the interview went.
Write down what went well, and what you could improve on.
Ideally, you will have access to a recording, so that you can
learn more about your performance. Always take the views of
your colleagues into account. There are few amongst us who
can listen to ourselves and not be over-critical.

Five-minute radio interview guide

- Find out about the station and the show in advance.

- Arrive in plenty of time.

- Be careful who you speak to.

- Listen to the station output while you are waiting.

- Follow the instructions from the station staff.

- Assume that the microphones are always on.

- Adjust the volume in your headphones.

- Use the cough button if necessary.

- Get your core message in early.

- Repeat your core message at the end.

- Leave your contact details.

- Jot down your notes as soon as the interview is over.

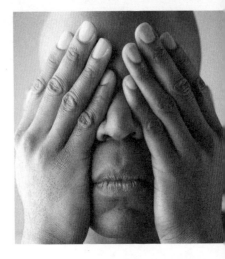
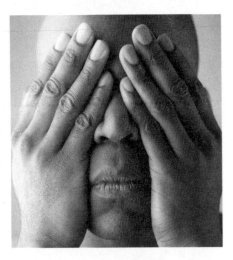
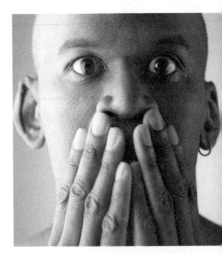

8 · Appearing on Television

It may well be that radio is superior to television because 'the pictures are better'. However, the visual aspects of television are of crucial importance, and you must understand how to use visual impact to best effect. Refer back to the chapters on appearance and body language before any television appearance, and check that you are looking your best.

Television magnifies every aspect of your appearance. Every gesture, grimace and half-smile is picked up by the camera, and may be used to illustrate a news item later on. Be aware that you may be on camera when someone else is talking (producers love a reaction shot), and even when you think the interview has ended. The golden rule is to imagine that you are always in view, and not to move until the floor manager tells you to.

Don't forget about the background. In the studio, you will have little control over what is around you, but on location, you should ensure that you are not filmed against a background that undermines your message. For example, if you are discussing how local traffic is causing severe noise problems, make sure that you aren't pictured against a backdrop of an empty road. Conversely, you can use a background to make your point. So if, in the previous

example, you have to keep shouting your answers as heavy
lorries thunder past, your point makes itself.

Types of TV interview

There are several different types of TV interview, and each
requires slightly different techniques. In every case, practice
and preparation is vital. If you arrive at an interview armed
with the knowledge that you can deal with the worst
possible question, you will have the confidence to perform at
your best.

TV interviews can be live or pre-recorded, on location or in-
studio, or (most tricky of all) down the line. To make things
slightly more complicated, pre-recorded interviews can be 'as
live', but we'll come back to that in a moment.

Let's have a look at each type of interview, and consider the
best way to prepare for and handle them.

Pre-recorded

There are two reasons for pre-recording TV interviews. One is
to be able to lift clips from it for a later news bulletin,
probably as part of a larger report. The second reason is to
use it in its entirety for later broadcast. The latter is known by
the term 'as live', because it is shot and replayed in real time.

Just as with radio interviews, the pre-recorded (known as 'pre-
rec') interview often follows a standard pattern. Before the
recording, the reporter will discuss the issues with you, and
may suggest particular themes or points that are worth
making. This is when you need to be careful. You must avoid
having words put in your mouth. You need to stick to your
prepared line, and make sure that you deliver your core
message.

Answering with the question – Remember that in most pre-recorded interviews, the questions asked by the reporter will not be heard. When you respond, you need to make sure that you repeat the gist of the question, so that the answer stands on its own as a valid clip or soundbite. Normally, the reporter will remind you of this, but if they forget, it is extremely frustrating to have to repeat the whole interview, particularly if you feel that you performed well. For example, if the reporter says, 'Why do you think that the situation is extremely volatile?', you must not respond by saying, 'I think it is because ...' since the viewer will have no idea what you are referring to. Instead, begin your answer by saying, 'The situation is extremely volatile because ...'

Of course, if you don't agree that it is volatile, don't be drawn into agreeing with the reporter!

Imagine it's live – When you are doing a pre-rec, you need to be at your best at all times. You will have little or no control over which response is edited out and used as a clip. It is possible for you to say, 'Can we do that one again?', and in almost every case, the reporter will agree. However, it may be that when the material is edited, particularly when reporters are working to a tight deadline, the 'wrong' clip (from your point of view) may be used. It is best, therefore, to treat even pre-recs as live interviews, correcting yourself if you make a mistake, and continuing regardless.

Making your point – The key thing to remember in a pre-rec is that the last question is often the most crucial. On most occasions, the reporter will suggest to you two or three key points that they would like you to summarise in a few seconds. This is the clip that they want to use, where your arguments are expressed in 15 to 20 seconds. Again, don't allow the reporter to suggest points that you are not comfortable making. However, you should have rehearsed and be prepared for the 'summary response'. This gives you the opportunity to make your key point in a memorable way, almost guaranteeing that this will be the 'money shot'.

Extra shots – After you have answered all of the questions, there will often be some more work to do. The reporter may ask you to help with the 'noddies'. These are the camera shots where the non-speaker is simply looking at the questioner and nodding to indicate that they are listening. They may also record the questions again, as 'reverses', possibly with the camera filming them over your shoulder.

These shots are then intercut with your answers to produce the final report. You may find the whole procedure a little odd, particularly if you haven't done a TV interview before. However, you need to follow the instructions of the reporter and camera operator, who have done this hundreds of times, and know what shots they need.

It may seem that the whole procedure is taking ages but reporters are always working to tight deadlines, so they won't waste your time. Don't forget to ask them when the item will appear.

Interview 'as live' – If the interview is shot 'as live', then the questions will be heard, so you don't need to repeat them as you answer. Indeed, it would sound odd and stilted if you did. You need to forget the fact that the interview is being recorded, and treat it as live. It may be that the interviewer, or the camera operator, may stop the recording. This can be particularly irritating if you are in full flow, delivering a perfect response, and the camera operator says 'I'm stopping, I can hear a plane coming.' Given the choice, always arrange to be filmed away from a flight path or busy railway line

Live on location
It is unusual to do a set-piece interview live on location, since the conditions and link may be unpredictable. It is much more usual for location interviews to be arbitrary 'vox pops', where passing strangers are pounced on and asked their opinion about a sporting event or pressing local issue.

If you find yourself doing an interview in the open air, make sure that you are dressed for comfort as well as style. You may have to wait around for several minutes in a freezing wind or driving rain. It is quite acceptable to refer to the conditions during your interview, and you will probably get an easier time if the interviewer can see that you are already suffering!

In-studio
TV studios can be daunting places for newcomers. There is a lot of technology, bright lights, and random activity going on, with several people apparently talking to themselves. Despite the glossy appearance on screen, much of the furniture is held together with sticky tape and string, as you will see when you sit behind it. I recall being on a breakfast TV show, behind a table with an appetising bowl of fruit and a glass of orange juice. As I sat down, the floor manager said to me, 'Don't drink the orange juice, it's coloured water. And the fruit is plastic.'

If you have a dry throat, ask for some (real) water. Have some throat sweets handy. If you find that your mouth still becomes dry, you can use the old actor's trick. Gently nip the inside of your cheek with your teeth, and you will find that your mouth becomes moist. Don't overdo it by biting too hard, since that will bring tears to your eyes as well.

There will be TV monitors around, showing various images. Don't look at them. There will be cameras moving around. Don't look at them. There will be a scrolling autocue script for the presenter to read. Don't look at it. Instead, look at the interviewer and forget everything else. When you are introduced, smile. Don't look shifty. Say hello and nod. If they make a mistake over your name or title, correct them politely.

Remember that you will need to be 'miked-up'.

The presenter will wear an ear piece. If they don't pay attention to you before the interview, bear in mind they may be receiving instructions from the gallery.

Down the line
A down-the-line TV interview is, for most people, the most difficult to master. There are remote studios in many towns and cities these days, which allow a live interview to be carried out without having to bring someone many miles to the main studio.

Often these remote studios are unstaffed, and you have to do a fair amount of set-up work yourself. Even in Broadcasting House in London, the original home of the BBC, you may be shown to the remote studio, let in to the room, and left to it. If you are luckier you will be helped by a technician, who will set everything up for you before the interview starts.

It isn't quite as daunting as it sounds. There is a notice on the wall explaining the procedure, and a phone number to call. You will be talked through the set-up process by a technician in the main studio, who will ensure that everything is working correctly.

Concentrating on the interview – Your focus will be the camera that is pointing at you. You need to look directly at it for the duration of your interview. If you look away, even for a moment, the viewer will perceive you as being less than totally honest, since it will appear to them that you can't 'look them in the eye'. The trick to this type of interview, then, is to maintain your gaze on the lens. Speaking to an inanimate object is not easy. For this reason, most presenters will imagine that they are talking to a trusted friend on the other side of the lens. If you can visualise a colleague, friend or family member that you enjoy talking to, imagine that you are speaking to them, and them alone, through the lens in front of you.

You will hear the interviewer's voice through a speaker. Don't look to where the voice is coming from, but keep focusing on the camera. If there is a monitor in the room, showing the interviewer in vision, it is almost impossible to ignore it. What you can do before the interview is to ask the technician if you can turn it off or turn it away from you. As a last resort, throw your coat over it.

Panel discussions

It may be a while before you appear on *Question Time*, but panel discussions are an important element of TV these days, and your first interview may well be as one of several studio guests.

A panel debate will be chaired by a presenter, who will introduce everyone and control the questioning. Talk directly to them, not to the other panel members. If an audience is present and asking questions, it may be appropriate to talk to them directly.

Stay calm at all times, even if you are being criticised by other panellists. If you lose your temper, you will probably lose the argument. Focus your response on their views, not on them personally. Don't interrupt anyone, but wait your turn. If you feel that an unfair comment has been made, ask if you can respond, even if the presenter is moving on to the next topic.

Who does what on TV

Researcher
The person who will have rung you beforehand to book you on the show. They'll be the person who collects you from reception on the day and offers you coffee.

Floor manager
Wears a head set and is the link with the gallery to the floor. The floor manager counts into and out of all links. If there's anything you need, talk to the floor manager.

Sound person
Will wire you up with a microphone, and check that you can be heard properly.

Camera operators
Usually there'll be three cameras for a studio shoot. Some studios now use remotely-operated cameras, which can be a little disconcerting.

Director
The person in the gallery who calls the shots on how the show looks. They are in overall control, or so they tell me.

Producer
The person in the gallery who calls the shots on editorial content. The producer is the person who'll have decided to have you on the show.

On the way to the studio
Make sure that you arrive in plenty of time for your appearance, bearing in mind that it will take a few minutes to reach the studio, via make-up and the green room. Always allow for travel delays, and keep the studio informed if you are running late. They probably won't re-schedule your interview, but will appreciate the information so that they can fill in with other items.

Make-up is necessary for all studio interviews, for both men and women. Just relax in the chair and let them get on with things. On your way home, drop in to the make-up room for a quick wipe with remover if you are feeling too conspicuous.

By all means take your notes with you so that you can remind yourself of your core message, but tuck them out of sight before you go into the studio.

In the green room
You will have a few minutes to wait before your appearance, and will be taken to the green room. There may be some snacks and drinks. It is unusual these days to find anything alcoholic, but if you do, avoid it.

If you need to visit the toilet, go early. Once someone comes to collect you, you won't have time to go, since you will be whisked into the studio in a matter of seconds.

There is usually a TV tuned to the programme you are due to appear on. It is a good idea to watch what is being discussed, since it may be useful to make a reference back to it in your interview.

If you are feeling nervous, take a few deep breaths. Concentrate on your core message, and visualise yourself returning to the green room after a successful appearance.

In the studio

If the studio is 'live', you will probably be taken to the edge of the backdrop to await your call, and then ushered in during an interval when a taped report is airing, or a presenter in a different part of the studio is talking. Take care not to trip over any cables, and be prepared for the sound technician to fit your mike.

When you are introduced, smile and nod at the interviewer, and off you go. It'll be over before you know it.

Using props

If you want to bring something into the studio with you – a new product that you are discussing, or your latest book – always ask first whether it will be acceptable. The producer will be concerned about camera shots, and since they can't talk to you directly, they may ask the interviewer to take the object from you, so that they can show it to the camera.

If you are pre-recording an interview, you may have the advantage of a rehearsal with a prop. This will allow you to practise the camera shots in advance. Of course, things still may not go to plan. For some years, I had a regular slot as a technology expert on a weekly TV show. Much of the show was devoted to new technology, which I would explain to the presenter. We often used to encounter what Dennis Norden used to call the 'OOPS' effect (Objects Only Perform Sometimes). If your demonstration goes horribly wrong, as mine did from time to time, the only thing to do is to make a joke of it and explain what it should have done.

In general, my advice would be to avoid using props.

After the interview
When the interview is over, stay in your seat until your microphone is removed and you are told that it is safe to go.

By the way, whatever the provocation, I would not recommend trying to storm out of an interview half-way through (doing a 'Nott' as it is known, after the example of a former UK government minister, who made a dreadful hash of trying to leave a TV interview, forgetting that he was still attached to the microphone cable). You may create quite a stir, but it is unlikely to help your case. It is better to stay put and keep calm (or at least look calm).

Make sure that you jot down your impressions as soon as the interview is over.

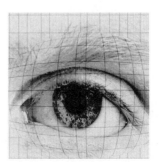

Five-minute TV interview guide

- Prepare well in advance.

- Take your notes with you, but tuck them out of sight.

- Think about your appearance, and ask someone to check you over.

- Arrive in plenty of time.

- If you need to use the toilet or have a drink, do it before you sit in the green room.

- Be ready for an instant call.

- Follow the floor manager's instructions.

- Look at the interviewer, not the camera.

- Get your core message in early.

- Stay still until you are told to move.

- Record your impressions.

9 · Other Media

An increasing number of ways of communicating a message are now becoming available, and are being driven by a number of factors.

The ubiquity of the Internet, and the increasing number of high-speed connections, means that video and audio communication direct to people's computers is now viable. An increasing number of companies are setting up services which provide programming, either to closed user groups or to the general public.

The cost of connections, equipment and supporting software is such that even the smallest organisation can become a broadcaster. The use of digital audio players has spawned the phenomenon of 'podcasting', where regular audio or video bulletins can be downloaded for later listening or viewing on a personal digital player. Even large broadcasting organisations have recognised that they have to start offering their services in different formats.

The reluctance of many people to travel to meetings and conferences in recent years has also encouraged the growth of new systems. It is extremely likely that you will find yourself using these systems, so now is the time to find out how to make the best impression.

Many of the techniques covered in this book are relevant to webchats, videoconferencing and the like. This chapter highlights the skills and knowledge that are specific to these emerging communication techniques, giving you the ability to deliver your core message via any medium.

Webchats

It is common nowadays for a radio or TV interview to be followed by a webchat, where Internet users pose questions, which appear in a small window on a computer screen, followed by the answers given by the interviewee. The technology to achieve this has been around for many years now, and the result is visually rather dull. The great advantage is that it can be viewed by thousands of Internet users simultaneously, with each one feeling that they are participating in an intimate debate.

Should you be asked to participate as a guest interviewee in a webchat, don't worry about your typing speed. You won't be keying in the answers yourself. Your job is to explain your answer, which will then be typed in by an operator. It is rather like having your answers translated into a foreign language, when you need to speak slowly, and allow pauses for the translator to finish.

The best analogy is a radio phone-in. If you have a friendly host, you will be offered a selection of questions, and allowed to pick the ones you wish to answer. Even if the webchat follows a radio or TV interview, don't assume that the participants have heard or seen it. Keep your answers concise, and make sure that you re-state your key message often.

Internet chat rooms have received a lot of bad publicity, much of which is justified. I would recommend that you only participate in webchats organised and monitored by well-known media organisations.

Teleconferences

Teleconferencing is an audio-only service usually accessed by telephone. Again, they are not new, and used to be known as conference calls. Many organisations now arrange teleconferences where an expert is interviewed, followed by a question-and-answer session in which any of the delegates can participate.

If you are asked to appear on a teleconference, you will probably be in a different location from your host. A certain amount of teleconferencing etiquette is required in order that all goes well.

Firstly, ensure that you are using a good-quality line. A mobile phone may be unreliable, and a speakerphone can sound very odd. It may be helpful to use a telephone headset, to keep your hands for making notes.

Secondly, make sure that you are somewhere that you won't be disturbed. Let colleagues or family know what you are doing, and how long the call is expected to last. Shut yourself in a room and put a note on the door. If you have another phone, unplug it or turn it off.

Thirdly, be aware of your audience. If the teleconference is being listened to worldwide, avoid idioms and analogies that are specific to one country. Speak slowly and clearly. If the host of the discussion is going to allow questions from the audience during the interview, that should be made clear at the beginning.

Make the same preparations that you would for any media interview. Have a drink handy, and spread your notes out in front of you, to avoid rustling papers. Keep a pen and some blank paper handy in case you need to jot down a complex question. To feel really secure, have a spare phone handy, although that may be going too far.

Video conferences

Video conferences may be conducted over a private, dedicated link, or over the Internet. Because you will be visible, refer back to chapter 4 (Your Personal Appearance). You will probably have the advantage of being able to see yourself on part of the screen, so that you can judge how you look. You will probably only need to worry about your head and shoulders, so don't take too much time choosing your shoes.

Although videoconferencing technology is improving, the video quality is not usually as good as television, and the 'refresh rate' of the images can be low. For this reason, avoid any sudden or quick movements. Allow for any transmission delays by pausing regularly.

Look at the camera when you are speaking, and refer to the tips in the previous chapter on television interviews which relate to down-the-line interviews. Speak in your normal voice.

Some videoconferencing systems are very sensitive to sound, and the camera will move to point at whoever is speaking. This is both a blessing and a curse, since a whispered aside may be picked up, and you may find yourself faced with a lens, having made a comment that you do not wish to repeat. If you are not speaking, you need to keep still and silent. There should be a mute button near your microphone. You should make full use of it.

Treat a video conference exactly as you would a TV interview, in a relaxed but professional manner.

10 · The Press Conference

If you ask a group of business people how they might publicise a new product or service, many of them will say 'Hold a press conference!' There may have been a time, many, many years ago, when journalists would attend all, or most of the press conferences that they were invited to. Those days, if indeed they ever existed, are long gone.

Nevertheless, press conferences are still important, and need to be organised and managed properly if they are to succeed. Every type of organisation holds press conferences for a wide variety of reasons. A football club may announce the appointment of a new manager, or acquisition of a new player. A campaigning organisation may launch an effort to change people's views about an environmental issue. The government may explain their new policy on transport. Whatever the issue, there is one common thread, and that is that every press conference must have a clear purpose, at least as far as the organisers are concerned.

Unfortunately, there is no way of controlling the questions that journalists may ask. If a retail company holds a press conference to announce the opening of a new superstore, but their annual report has just shown a huge drop in profits, there will be only one topic of questioning.

The key to success, as ever, is good and thorough preparation.

When to hold a press conference

If you decide that a press conference is appropriate, timing is important. Of course, if a disaster has occurred, the timing will be forced upon you to some extent.

You want to ensure that stories appear in the media. Knowledge of deadlines is therefore vital. There is no point holding a press conference on a Friday if you want the story to appear in the review section of Sunday's newspaper, as it will be too late to include the story. For weekly journals, you need to be aware of their final copy date, and hold the conference a few days in advance of it.

Check whether any other press conferences are scheduled at the same time (the easiest way is to ask a journalist whether they have had any other invitations). Unless you can provide the major draw, re-schedule your conference.

If you are expecting radio or TV journalists to attend, organise your conference in the morning, to give the opportunity of coverage on both the lunchtime and evening bulletins.

The venue

Indoors is always preferable, at least in the UK. It provides more certainty over the conditions, and gives the technicians somewhere to plug in their equipment. Make sure that it is somewhere accessible, with easy parking nearby. It is more important that journalists turn up than that the event makes a statement by using an unusual venue.

If you are not sure about numbers, err on the side of a smaller, rather than larger, room. A crowded press event looks far more impressive than a half-empty one. Visit the venue a few days before to make sure that it is suitable. On the day, arrive a couple of hours early to guarantee that everything is set up correctly.

The agenda

It is usual to begin by making a statement, which you have also thoughtfully handed out to the press in advance. Thank your audience for attending, and then make your main point. Keep your remarks brief, since no one wants to listen to a long speech. A question-and-answer session can then follow. (See chapter 11 for some tips on how to handle tricky questions.)

Broadcast journalists are looking for a soundbite, so they may well wait until the end of the event, and ask you to do a brief interview. You may even be invited to the studio later on for a live debate.

Organisation tips

Make sure that everyone involved knows their responsibilities and is clear about the message. I still remember in great detail a press conference that I helped to organise, when the director declined to have a briefing. The conference began with a statement from the director, in which they said exactly the opposite of our agreed core message, much to the amazement of the other speakers.

Even if radio and TV stations have not responded to your invitation, call them again early on the day (around 8.30am is fine), before their morning meeting. They may decide to send someone after all.

Expect most people to either reject the invitation, or not arrive. It is notoriously difficult to fill a press conference. If you receive only a couple of confirmations, cancel the event, and send out a press pack instead.

If a newspaper declines to send a reporter, call the photo desk and ask if a photographer can attend. A picture and a caption may be more valuable than a story.

Make sure to collect the details of everyone who attends.

Taking questions
Someone needs to be responsible for chairing the conference, so that the questions are dealt with in a sensible manner. It will be obvious if certain topics are being avoided, so you need to be prepared to take on any issue that arises. Of course, you should have rehearsed your answers in advance, and prepared for the worst, so you shouldn't get caught out.

Respond truthfully. You will be in a semi-public forum, where all your words are recorded, and may be used on news bulletins. If you try to hide information, evade issues, or make a statement which later is found out to be untrue, it will come back to haunt you.

The important thing about press conferences is that they give you the chance to put your side of the story, so make the most of the opportunity.

Five-minute press conference guide

■ Do you really need a press conference? Would a press statement be just as useful? (Or saying nothing at all?)

■ Decide the purpose of the event, and make sure everyone agrees.

■ Check the venue, and make the arrangements well in advance.

■ Make sure that the date and time fits in with media deadlines.

■ Aim to have at least 75 per cent of the seats filled.

■ Re-check with radio and TV stations early in the morning.

■ If very few people are coming, cancel the event and talk to reporters individually.

■ Make sure that everyone understands their role, and what they will say.

■ Rehearse answers to all likely questions.

■ Keep a list of all attendees.

■ Allow time for post-event interviews.

■ Record your impressions, and have a feedback session.

11 · Handling Questions

This is probably the most important chapter in this book. If you can learn how to handle questions confidently, you will be able to cope in any situation. It is the most natural thing in the world, since whenever we are in conversation we are either asking or answering questions. On the face of it, then, it should not present a problem. However, the greatest fear that people have when appearing on the media is that they will be asked questions that they cannot answer, or that might embarrass them.

There are some simple techniques that you can use to deal with any type of question, whether it is complex, ill-informed or downright hostile. This chapter will explain them. Most importantly, you need to remember that you are the expert. In most cases, your interviewer will know very little about the topic, and may only have read the first line of your press release. You therefore have a great advantage. If you are unsure about something, preface it by the phrase, 'In my opinion ...'

Being an expert
Many of us don't think of ourselves as experts. Sometimes we need to learn that we really are. A few years ago, I was a weekly guest on Sky Business News. I used to discuss new technology, usually in conversation with Michael Wilson, the business editor. To and from the studios, I had the same

driver every week, a friendly chap called Dave. One day, my mobile phone rang while I was in the back of the car. It was Geoffrey Boycott, calling from South Africa, where he was commentating on a test match. He was having problems with a new laptop, and wanted to ask my advice about how to use a particular programme. I was able to help him out, to Dave's amusement. An hour later, after I had finished my TV interview, I went to the green room to wait for Dave to pick me up. George Best was there. He came over, shook hands and introduced himself. He said, 'You're Alan Stevens, aren't you?' I nodded. 'I just watched your interview,' he said. 'Can I ask your advice about buying a new PC?' On the way back to the office, I related this encounter to Dave, and said how stunned I was that two of my sporting heroes had sought my advice in the space of a couple of hours. 'Ah,' said Dave, 'that's because you're an expert.'

You are an expert in your field too. You should always remember that when you are being interviewed. Avoid using abbreviations or jargon, unless you explain the meaning (and then why use it?). Keep your answers brief and concise, so that they can be used as clips in later bulletins. Don't forget your core message. By all means, use examples and anecdotes to give human interest to your responses.

Anticipating the worst
Preparation is the key to handling questions. It is not possible to anticipate every possible question, but if you have planned properly, then nothing will catch you out.

In order to prepare, you should first consider the source of the questions. Will they be put to you by a single interviewer, by a studio audience, or by callers on a phone-in show? Also consider the type of programme, and who it is aimed at. If you are talking to a media professional, they will be asking the sort of questions that their viewers and listeners would like to put to you. Very often, your interview will have been trailed for several hours beforehand, and questions will have been submitted in advance. You need to understand the concerns of your audience so that your answers are relevant to them.

Your friends and colleagues will be able to help you draw up a list of questions. You should make sure that you ask them, 'If you were the interviewer, what would you ask me that I might not be able to answer?' Tell them not to hold back, or be kind to you. You want to hear the most difficult question that might arise. Believe me, they will be able to come up with some, since they know exactly which skeletons are in which cupboards. Of course, you now need them to do a little more, which is to help you come up with good answers.

If you know that you can cope with the worst questions, you will be confident, relaxed and more focused.

Respecting the questioner

Staying calm is very important. There is no such thing as a stupid question, and you should always show respect to your questioner. It can be difficult, especially if you know that the questioner has a particular bias. Even worse, they may make remarks which you find irritating. You must keep calm, and ignore any unpleasantness. Answer the question directly and factually, without being drawn into criticising someone else's opinion.

Never use sarcasm, or belittle the questioner. If you do, onlookers will side with the questioner, not you. Focus on what they have said, not on them. If you disagree strongly with their stance, say something like, 'I understand your point of view, but I don't share it. Let me explain how I see things ...' Don't make any assumptions. Simply accept the questioner's presuppositions, correcting them gently if necessary.

Always smile, and thank the questioner for making their point. Even if you are seething with rage and indignation inside, don't show it. You will win far more respect if you maintain a professional image.

How to rehearse

You need to practise your responses, in terms of both content and style. Once you are happy that you have considered the most likely questions, ask a friend or colleague to take on the role of the interviewer. Give them a list of questions to ask, but encourage them to make up some of their own as well.

Ideally, have someone else watch both of you, so that they can give you feedback on your performance. If you have access to a video camera, you can use that to record and assess your responses.

The idea is not to deliver carefully scripted answers. You will sound false if you do. You should use your normal conversational style, and aim to get your core message across. Don't be afraid to admit that you don't know something which is outside your area of expertise, but do offer to find out.

Listen to what your colleagues have to say, and adjust your answers accordingly.

The importance of listening

Listen carefully, right to the end of the question. There is often a temptation to formulate a response while the questioner is still speaking. This often stems from a desire to appear to be very knowledgeable, by not even having to pause for thought before answering.

If you are taking part in a debate in front of an audience, and you are answering a question which is preceded by a story, or it is clear that the questioner has several points to make, it is quite acceptable to take notes, to make sure that you cover all of their points. Don't just write down the question, but also jot down a few key words to use in your reply.

A questioner may include several points, effectively asking several different questions. Consider for a moment, and then offer an answer to the easiest one. Of course, you don't tell the questioner that. Instead you say, 'Let me take your second question first.' Deliver a full response, and then say, 'Remind me of your other points.' More often than not, they will ask you to move on, or will have forgotten what else they asked.

Using pauses

You need to take your time, and fully comprehend what the questioner is seeking before you start to reply. There is nothing wrong with taking a few seconds to consider how to respond. You might immediately say, 'Good question,' or 'Interesting point,' to give yourself a little more time, but it is more important to give a considered, full response than a quick, partial one.

You can also use the tactic of asking for a question to be repeated to buy yourself some more thinking time. Don't over-use this trick, but reserve it for the time when you really need it.

Dealing with hostility

Do not assume that a question is hostile because it is asked in a hostile way. Separate the content of the question from the manner in which it is asked.

There is a very effective technique known as 'neutral rephrasing' which you can use to remove the hostility from questions. It works like this. If someone asks a very hostile question, possibly using strong language, you say, 'Let me see if I understand what you are asking.' Then rephrase the question they have asked, but using non-hostile terms. Imagine the question is, 'You're hopeless. You clearly haven't got the faintest idea about the issues here, and you sound like a complete idiot. What can an ill-informed person like you possibly have to offer?' You reply by saying, 'Thank you for the question. Let me see if I understand your point. You suspect that I don't fully understand the situation here, and therefore may not be able to help. Let me explain what I know, how I came to my conclusions, and why I think they represent the correct approach.' You then answer the question as fully as possible.

It is very hard for someone to keep generating hostility if you remain calm. However, if you try to match aggression with aggression, everything can spiral out of control. The more hostile your questioner becomes, the calmer you should be.

Avoidance tactics

There may be some topics that you do not wish to discuss at all. You need to use tactics that deflect the question without appearing evasive.

If you are facing a persistent interviewer, it may not be a comfortable experience. BBC stalwart Jeremy Paxman once asked the former Conservative Home Secretary, Michael Howard, the same question twelve times. Mr Howard declined to answer twelve times, and the interview is now regarded as a benchmark of persistence.

There are a number of ways that you can steer away from an awkward topic. You can admit ignorance, but offer to find out. You can explain that you are not an expert in that particular area (a tricky one if that is why you are being interviewed). You can point out that the matter is either confidential or *sub judice*. You can treat the question as a joke ('Good try – you know we can't talk about that.'). Probably the most effective tactic of all is to offer an answer about a related topic. None of these would work with Jeremy Paxman, but let's hope you are never in his firing line.

Six things you should never say to a journalist

So much for answering questions. Here, as a reminder of what not to do, is a list of six things you should never say.

1. *'This is off the record.'*
A phrase which will make the reporter carefully note everything that you say, and reproduce it to your acute embarrassment.

2. *'I don't think you'll be able to understand this, so I'll try to say it as simply as possible.'*

Never ever talk down to a reporter. They know when they're being patronised.

3. 'I've never heard of your radio show/TV programme.'
More often than not, this will be true, but local reporters grow up to be national reporters and if you treat them well, you'll remain a handy contact in their little black book.

4. 'We're the best in the business.'
As soon as the reporter leaves, they'll check up on your rivals to see whether you're boasting.

5. 'We've had fantastic press reviews in the States.'
Journalists prefer to make their own minds up. Being told that they should copy their overseas colleagues is not a good idea.

6. 'No comment.'
A popular one this, which leads to one of two possible outcomes: 'XYZ Ltd declined to confirm or deny rumours that ...' or 'XYZ Ltd refused point-blank to talk to us about ...' Neither of these is good news for you.

Five-minute guide to handling questions

■ Remember that you are an expert.

■ Prepare for the worst.

■ Be brief.

■ Be honest.

■ Ask for clarification.

■ Don't feel that you have to answer every question.

■ Separate multiple questions, and answer the easiest part first.

■ Stay calm.

■ Use neutral rephrasing to defuse hostility.

■ Always show respect to the questioner.

12 · Dealing with a Crisis

I hope that you won't need the advice in this chapter, but if you do, there are some basic things to remember about dealing with the media in a crisis.

Firstly, the media cannot be ignored. If something goes wrong, they will find out, and they will be seeking a statement from you as quickly as possible.

Secondly, if you do not talk to the media quickly, someone else will. It is far better for you to be stating your authoritative view than for speculation to come from another source.

Thirdly, you need to be prepared. There will be no time for media training when the press are at your front door. Many companies have a disaster recovery plan which protects their employees and data, but not their reputation. You need to be certain that there is always someone available who is media-ready. Having procedures is not the same as being prepared. Practice is crucial.

Your practical crisis management procedures are not for discussion here. I'm assuming that they are in place, have been tested, and work well. This chapter will focus on how to handle the media if disaster strikes.

Recognising a crisis

In order to react quickly, you need to know that a crisis has occurred. This means having good internal communications in place, especially out of hours. For some reason, most crises seem to occur at the most inconvenient times.

It is likely that the media will contact you before you approach them. If the media call is the first knowledge that you receive of a crisis, never admit as much. Always stall for time, by explaining that you are trying to find out as much as possible, and that you will be more than willing to talk to them soon.

Acting quickly

As mentioned above, you need to be ready to deal with a crisis at very short notice. By acting quickly and being proactive, you will reduce the amount of rumour and speculation which would otherwise appear in the media.

Gather your key decision-makers and spokespeople together as fast as you can, which may well be by using a telephone conference in the first instance. Set up a contact point for the media, and make the details widely known. Make sure that you use a different contact point for the media and for enquiries from friends and relations.

As media spokesman for a large organisation, I once received a call late on a Sunday evening, telling me that one of our websites was revealing thousands of credit card numbers and customer details. By six o'clock Monday morning, I was in the BBC studios in London, ready to be grilled on the breakfast news. I spent the rest of the day in radio and TV studios, completing over 30 interviews by the evening. I explained our position, detailed the immediate action we had taken, and promised that no one would lose money as a result.

I believe that the prompt action defused the crisis, and saved the reputation of the organisation. You don't have to take my word for that, since the video of that breakfast TV interview is now being used by media training companies worldwide to show how you should respond to a crisis.

It is likely that your senior staff will be doorstepped and ambushed by reporters. Having a bright light shone in your eyes and a microphone thrust into your face as you leave your house in the morning is disconcerting at the best of times. If you are already under pressure because of your concern about what has happened, you may say something that you later regret. The only way to prepare for this is to have your senior staff trained to cope with the eventuality, as part of your disaster recovery procedure. In my view, nothing can prepare you for this type of intrusion unless you have gone through the experience and learned how to cope with it.

Doing the right things

You need to make information available as soon as possible. At first, this will be to confirm that an incident has occurred, and to make it clear that you are doing everything possible to resolve matters. If the incident is serious, the emergency services may be involved. If so, liaise with them to find out what, if anything, they are saying to the press.

It is likely that you will need to hold a press conference at short notice. Refer to chapter 10 for tips on what to do, but bear in mind that saying something to the press early is better than holding an immaculately-staged press conference a couple of days later. The press and the public will be hungry for information, and it is your job to supply what you can.

Though a press conference may be important, make sure that it does not impinge on other activities. Your senior staff will be there as spokespeople, so make a point of keeping the conference short, which also shows how urgently you are dealing with the crisis.

What to say, what not to say

Never, ever speculate about the cause of a problem. Inevitably, one of the first questions asked by a reporter will be, 'Do you know what caused this?' Even if you have a good idea what happened, always say, 'It's too early to tell.'

Levels of importance

Your main concern should be, and no doubt will be, the welfare of any people involved. If there are injuries, or worse, deaths, your thoughts and statements will always be about your concerns for the victims. There is a hierarchy of issues that you should talk about in the aftermath of any crisis. People come first, environment second, property third and money last. All of your verbal and written statements should follow this pattern.

Taking it seriously

Your most senior staff should be the spokespeople. For one thing, they should be used to dealing with the media. More significantly, it sends out a signal that your organisation is treating the crisis seriously, and not leaving it to junior staff to sort out. If your managing director is unavailable for interview, possibly because they are overseas, you should ensure that they have at least made a comment that you can give to the press. If the crisis is urgent enough, they will also have to abandon their plans and return home. Nothing is worse than a story about a company in crisis, accompanied by pictures of the managing director lounging on a beach.

Never lie to a reporter. Trying to cover up an incident will simply set up the conditions for another crisis, this time damaging your organisation's credibility, not to mention yours. If you don't know the answer to a question, say so, but explain that you are trying to find out.

Legal advice
It is wise to take legal advice as soon as possible, to ensure that you do not make any statements that could cause problems later on. Of course, the most important piece of advice will be not to admit liability. By all means express your feelings and concerns, but do not place yourself in a position that could later cause huge embarrassment, and costs. Even if you believe that the problem is your fault, you may be wrong, so don't make an admission of guilt.

Working with others
If there are several organisations involved, make sure that you liaise with them as quickly as possible, and decide who is going to take the lead in dealing with the press. The last thing that you want is several different press briefings saying different things. Unfortunately, you may find yourself in the position where another organisation is trying to distance itself from the problems, and put the blame on you. Don't be drawn into any discussions about responsibility, and steer clear of criticising any other organisation. Instead, say that you are keen to work with everyone involved to mitigate the impact of the crisis as soon as is practical.

Becoming the definitive source
All sorts of people may be offering their views to reporters, including witnesses, other workers, unions, police and industry experts. You need to establish your organisation, and your spokespeople, as the most important source of information.

In this age of 24-hour rolling news coverage, a story will develop very quickly, and gather its own momentum. Reporters will try to find as many different sources as possible, to build up a picture of what has occurred. You can enlist the media's help to make sure that you are the key source, by offering them information before they seek it out.

Do not assume that the media will be hostile to you, or looking to blame you for causing the problems. To begin with, it is likely that they will be sympathetic, or at worst, neutral. Make spokespeople available, and accept all requests for interview if you possibly can. If you try to ignore the media, the words, 'We asked a representative of XYZ for an interview, but they declined to comment,' will create an impression that you may have something to hide.

The stake-out
If the crisis continues for several days, your staff may become victims of the media stake-out. It may mean that you and they have to pass through a media throng on the way to and from your business.

Remember that you need to keep your staff informed too, and provide them with guidance about talking to the media. Explain that there is a media contact point, through which all media contact should be channelled. If your staff make comments to the press about the lack of information they have received, it will affect your reputation for openness.

Correcting misreporting
Monitor the media, and immediately counter any erroneous statements or misinformation. There may be a great deal of speculation in the press, but it should stay within the realm

of 'fair comment'. If you feel that a serious mistake has been made, seek a retraction and a correction.

Don't overlook the impact of the Internet. Someone should be given the task of monitoring websites and Internet discussion groups. It may not be possible to force people to withdraw online comments, but you need to know as much as possible about what is being said. It is quite acceptable to use this knowledge in interviews, by saying, 'We are aware of the allegations that are being made on the Internet, and this is our reaction ...'

After the crisis is over

You don't need me (I hope) to tell you that you should conduct a thorough review of all your procedures after the crisis has passed.

There is another opportunity to generate good media coverage, though. If you have handled the crisis well, call a media outlet that has covered the story, and offer them an interview about what happened, and the lessons that have been learnt.

Always use your media relationships to good effect, in good times and bad times. Journalists are your friends.

Five-minute crisis checklist

- Recognise that a crisis has occurred.

- Act quickly.

- Set up a media contact point.

- Provide as much information as possible, but don't speculate.

- Senior staff must be spokespeople.

- Accept all interview requests.

- Ensure that you are the definitive source of information.

- Make sure that your staff are fully prepared and informed.

- Monitor the media, including the Internet.

- Correct any misreporting.

- Offer a positive story after it is all over.

Appendix

Blank checklists

Five-minute preparation checklist

Type of interview (live, pre-recorded, print)............................

Medium (radio, TV, print, Internet)..

Media outlet (station or publication)......................................

Journalist ....

Contact number ....

Phone call or in person ....

Venue...

Time...

Arrangements (e.g. car pickup) ....

....

....

....

Message sheet completed?..

Use the form above to ensure that you are aware of all necessary arrangements. In addition, you will need the Core Message Guide (see chapter 2) to ensure that you have planned what you are going to say.

Backgrounder checklist

Organisation name ....

Main activities ....

....

....

When established...

Number of employees ....

Financial information (turnover etc).....................................

....

Locations...

....

....

Key people ....

....

Significant products/services ....

....

Recent announcements ....

Core message planner checklist

Message 1 ....
Keep? Y/N

Message 2 ....
Keep? Y/N

Message 3 ....
Keep? Y/N

Audience

Type of interview ....

Date .... Time ....

Interviewer ....

TV/radio station ....

Description of likely audience ....

....

....

Final core message ....

....

....

Index

If you want to know how... to boost sales and profits through seminars and workshops

'In this book, owners of small businesses will discover a proactive, exciting, profitable and proven formula for increasing sales. It will show you specifically;

- Why Seminar Selling can be a key to significant growth and profits
- The considerable benefits to all small businesses – not just white collar-sectors
- The benefits to attendees of your seminars
- How to plan, prepare, market and host your seminars
- The special presentation skills needed to deliver your business messages with power, clarity, confidence, conviction and impact
- How to follow up afterwards
- Extra ideas to help you maximise profits

Seminar Selling today is about the skilful combination of a variety of traditional and modern sales and marketing techniques and I hope this book will empower you to discover and exciting, creative, proactive and incredibly profitable new direction for your business.' **Philip Calvert**

Successful Seminar Selling
The ultimate small business guide to producing sales and profits through seminars and workshops
Philip Calvert

'Without effective promotion of your product or service, no-one will know you exist. This book is ideal for small business owners as it reveals one of the most profitable ways of promoting your company – seminar selling.' – **Digby Jones, Director-General, Confederation of British Business**

'The ideas and tips in this book are invaluable and will add not only confidence to any speaker, but additional income streams to any business.' – **Frank Furness, International Motivational Speaker**

ISBN 1 85703 966 1

If you want to know how... to get free publicity for your event

If your company, club, church or charity has a story to tell or something new, free or amazing to offer, journalists want to hear from you.

Getting Free Publicity
Secrets of Successful press relations
Pam and Bob Austin

This step-by-step manual takes you right through from who you should target and what journalists are looking for, to practical suggestions for choosing and presenting stories that will get accepted by editors You will discover how to write effective press releases and articles, how to deal with media interviews – and what to do if a journalist gets your story wrong.

ISBN 1 85703 972 6

How To Books are available through all good bookshops, or you can order direct from us through Grantham Book Services.

Tel: +44 (0)1476 541080
Fax: +44 (0)1476 541061
Email: orders@gbs.tbs-ltd.co.uk

Or via our website

www.howtobooks.co.uk

To order via any of these methods please quote the title(s) of the book(s) and your credit card number together with its expiry date.

For further information about our books and catalogue, please contact:

How To Books
3 Newtec Place
Magdalen Road
Oxford OX4 1RE

Visit our web site at

www.howtobooks.co.uk

Or you can contact us by email at info@howtobooks.co.uk